Thomas Cook Publishing

PRAGUE

BY

LOUIS JAMES

Produced by
Thomas Cook Publishing

Written by Louis James

Original photography by Jon Wyand

Edited and designed by Laburnum Technologies
Pvt Ltd, C-533 Triveni Apts, Sheikh Sarai Phase 1,
New Delhi 110017

Published by Thomas Cook Publishing
A division of Thomas Cook Holdings Ltd

PO Box 227, The Thomas Cook Business Park,
Units 19–21, Coningsby Road,
Peterborough PE3 8XX, United Kingdom
E-mail: books@thomascook.com
www.thomascookpublishing.com

ISBN: 1-841572-42-X

Managing Director: Kevin Fitzgerald

Publisher: Donald Greig

Series Consultant: Vivien Stone

Printed and bound in Spain by: Grafo Industrias Gráficas, Basauri

Cover: Astronomical clock of the Town Hall, Old Town Square, Prague.
Photograph by Antony Souter.
Inside cover: photographs supplied by Spectrum Colour Library

CD manufacturing services provided by business interactive ltd, Rutland, UK

Contents

Introduction

The 'Golden City', the 'City of a Hundred Spires', the 'Paris of the Thirties': Prague (Praha) has inspired any number of flattering and romantic descriptions. It wears such laurels lightly, since its mixture of beauty and an atmosphere soaked in history speaks for itself.

Prague, it is often said, lies at the heart of Europe. Under its first ruling dynasty, the Přemyslids, and still more under the first three Luxembourg kings of Bohemia (1310–1419), it rose to be the focus of a great Central European empire. It reached its apogee of wealth and splendour under Charles IV (1346–78), who was also elected Holy Roman Emperor.

Mosaic in the Emmaus Monastery
(Klášter Emauzy)

All this began to fall apart when the violent religious struggles of the 15th century between the followers of the reformer Jan Hus and Catholic rulers split the country. The Hussite wars also sharpened the age-old conflict between Germans (occupying many of the most influential offices of church and state) and native Slavs. In fact, Prague had been a twin-cultured city, Slavic and Germanic, ever since Otakar II invited Germans to colonise his new town of Malá Strana in 1257. It remained so up to the 20th century, with German domination being the basis of the Habsburg rule between 1526 and 1918. A third, deeply influential cultural element was supplied by the Jews who, though they number only about 2,000 today, formed 25 per cent of the city's population in 1700. Finally, the Roma (gypsy) minority, although still largely ignored, has always been an important part of the city's population. Recognition of their place in society was a precondition to the Czech Republic's acceptance into the European Union.

Despite being washed over by so many conflicts – dynastic, religious, racial – Prague has remained one of the world's best preserved cities. Here, as nowhere else, you may drink beer in one of dozens of Romanesque and Gothic cellars, wander around some of the finest Gothic and Baroque churches in Europe, or track down unique exotic examples of Art Nouveau or Cubist architecture. The people of Prague, having lived through wars and oppression, have earned a reputation for resourcefulness on the one hand, resilience and doggedness on the other. The hero of the novel, *The Good Soldier Švejk*, represents the former quality;

playwright and statesman Václav Havel, with his determination to 'live in truth', embodies the latter.

Prague today has come alive after 40 years of Communist gloom. Over a decade after the 'changes', the city has been transformed. Its marvellous musical tradition continues, artistic and cultural activity is as vibrant as ever, and its legacy of hundreds of beautiful buildings and monuments has been renovated.

Strolling in Old Town Square (Staré Město)

The City

Prague

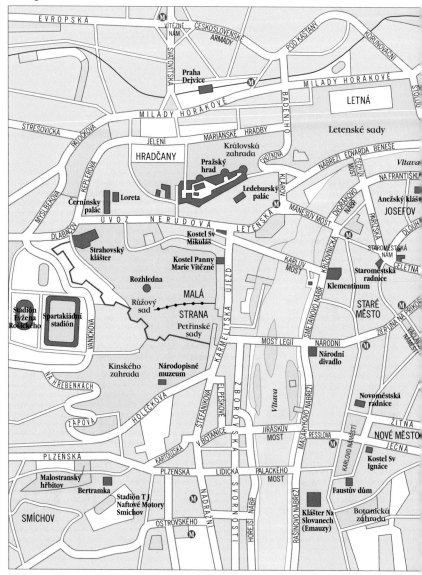

'... *the most beautiful inland town in Europe.*'
ALEXANDER, BARON VON HUMBOLDT

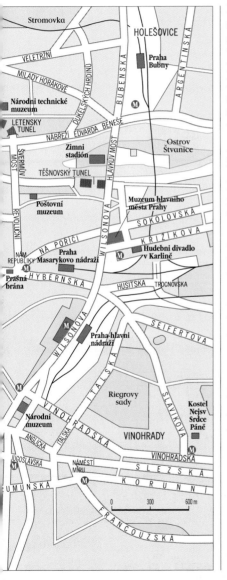

Prague lies 50 degrees 5 minutes north, and 14 degrees 25 minutes east – a city at the centre of Europe, but part of both Western and Eastern European culture. Its topography is determined by the River Vltava. The 497sq km conurbation stretches 48km along both banks of the river, a huge expansion from the modest town of 1883 (8.5sq km).

Like Rome, Prague is built on seven hills. On the left (western) bank of the Vltava, the wedge-shaped plateau called Hradčany rises abruptly from a narrow ribbon of land along the shore. One of the four great cities of Central Europe (the other three being Vienna, Cracow, and Budapest), Prague lay on important trade routes crossing Europe from Germany, Poland, Russia, and the East.

The toll levied on the Judith Bridge across the Vltava brought in revenue for the crown: the town benefited from the supply of goods and services. The construction of the Charles Bridge in 1357 was a practical necessity, since flood waters had all but swept away its predecessor. While the original inhabitants of Prague had chosen the better protected slopes above the west bank for their dwellings, flooding on the east side continued until the late 13th century. The problem was partially solved by raising the street level in Staré Město (Old Town). Systematic regulation of the Vltava had to wait until the 19th century.

Areas of Prague

'Prague is actually composed of two

parts. To the right of the Vltava is the Old Town – the Prague of Franz Kafka, the Prague of the Jewish community, the Prague of the Hussites, Czech Prague. To the left of the Vltava is the Lesser Quarter – the Baroque, the Catholic Prague, the Prague of the Counter-Reformation with its palaces of the nobility, with its many churches and monasteries.'

Barbara Coudenhove Kalergi

It was only in 1784 that the Emperor Joseph II ordered the four historic towns of Prague – Hradčany and Malá Strana (the Lesser Quarter) on the west bank of the Vltava, and Staré Město and Nové Město (the Old and New Towns) on the east bank – to be merged into a single municipality. Josefov, the Jewish ghetto, was amalgamated with Staré Město in 1850. Except for a large slice of Nové Město, these historic areas today constitute Prague's First District.

Most of historic Prague, and, there-fore, most tourist sights, are located in Praha 1. The modern capital is divided for administrative purposes into a total of 13 districts. These are the result of five further phases of expansion after 1784. The last period of growth of residential and industrial suburbs occurred in 1974.

Climate

Prague's climate is dictated by a mixture of oceanic and continental influences. The average temperature of 9°C implies a mild climate, but it can be very hot in summer (May–September), while in winter (November–March) the temperature stays at or well below zero.

Thomas Cook's Prague
When the state of Czechoslovakia was created after World War I, Thomas Cook began actively to promote tours to Prague and the surrounding countryside. In 1922 the *Thomas Cook Travellers Gazette*, founded in 1851, carried an article promoting the spas and health resorts of Czechoslovakia and describing Prague as one of the most attractive cities on the Continent.

The city is a study in architectural styles; facing page: the Old Town Square is a focal meeting place

History

8th century AD	Libuše, a legendary princess, has a vision of a city on the river, to be built where a man is found constructing the threshold (*práh*) to his house. In a subsequent vision she sees a young ploughman (*přemysl*) who will marry her and found the Přemyslid line.
Late 9th century	Duke Bořivoj I, the first historically verified Přemyslid, founds a citadel (Hradčany) on the Vltava.
Tradition says 929, but more likely 935	Duke Wenceslas (later to become patron saint of Bohemia) is murdered by his brother, Boleslav I.
1085	Vratislav II is made first King of Bohemia by Emperor Henry IV.
1257	Otakar II settles German merchants and artisans in the new town of Malá Strana.
1306	The Přemyslid dynasty dies out.
1346	Prague's golden age begins with the accession of Charles IV of the Luxembourg dynasty. In 1355 he is crowned Holy Roman Emperor. Charles Bridge, St Vitus' Cathedral, Karlštejn, and the Týn Church are built.
1348	Nové Město and the Charles University (Karolinum) are founded.

St Augustine, on the Charles Bridge

1357	Construction of the Charles Bridge aids development on the east bank of the Vltava.
1415	Jan Hus, the religious reformer, is burned alive for heresy at the Council of Constance.
1419	First defenestration of Prague: Hussites throw councillors from the windows of the New Town Hall.
1458–71	The Hussite king George of Poděbrady rules in Bohemia.
1483	Second defenestration of Prague: the mayor is thrown from the windows of the Old Town Hall.
1526	Ferdinand I becomes the first Habsburg king of Bohemia. He brings the Jesuits to Prague in 1556.
1576–1611	Rudolf II invites scholars, artists, and astronomers to his Prague court, among them Tycho Brahe and Johannes Kepler.
1618	The third and most famous defenestration of Prague takes place: Protestant nobles throw Ferdinand II's councillors from the windows of Prague castle. This triggers the Thirty Years War.

A window on history: scene of the famous 1618 defenestration of Prague

1620 The Bohemian
Protestants are defeated at
the Battle of the White
Mountain, and the
Counter-Reformation is
driven forward. Fine
churches and palaces are
built, but Prague is
reduced to a backwater of
the Habsburg Empire.

1740–80 Maria Theresa introduces
enlightened reforms, but
tries to expel the Jewish
population from
Prague.

1784 The four Prague
towns of Hradčany, Malá
Strana, Staré Město,
and Nové Město are
amalgamated. Joseph II
allows freedom of
religion and abolishes
serfdom, but
enforces

German as the language
of state.

1790–1848 The rise of Czech
national consciousness
culminates in the
unsuccessful revolution of
1848.

1861 The first Czech mayor of
Prague is elected, leading
to increasing tension
between Czechs and
Germans.

1918 At the end of World
War I, the Republic of
Czechoslovakia is
founded. The architect of
Czech independence,
Tomáš Masaryk, is its first
president.

Statue in
Wenceslas Square

NEDEJ-ZAHYNOUTI-NÁM-I-BUDOUCÍM

Memorial to victims of repressions, Wenceslas Square

1939	Prague's Jews are sent to concentration camps.
1948	The Communist Party takes power.
1968	The 'Prague Spring', led by Alexander Dubček, is crushed by the Warsaw Pact invasion.
1989	The Communist regime collapses on 10 December. On 29 December Václav Havel is elected president.
1990	Following elections in June, a right-of-centre government is formed, and begins the transformation of Czechoslovakia into a market economy.
1993	On 1 January, the Czech and Slovak Republics formally separate. Prague is the capital of the new Czech Republic.
1996	In January, Prime Minister Václav Klaus announces the Czech Republic's application to join the European Union.
1997	The Czechs prepare their entry into the European Union and accept formal entry into NATO.
2004	Tentative EU entry date.

Governance

In the 19th century, Prague became the focus of the Czech national revival led by the distinguished historian František Palacký (1798–1876). Palacký refused to take part in the German National Assembly held in Frankfurt during the 1848 revolution against the reactionary Habsburg government, presiding over a Pan-Slav Congress in Prague instead; an unmistakable signal that the days of German political and cultural domination were numbered.

Protest and patriotism on the streets: faces painted with the Czech flag

The Republic

The man who realised Palacký's dream was Tomáš Garrigue Masaryk (1850–1937) (*see p101*). During World War I, Masaryk, in exile in the USA, persuaded the allies to recognise a new (Slavic) Czechoslovak state in the event of victory. On 28 October 1918, the Czechoslovak Republic was declared in Prague with Masaryk as president. The Slovaks soon grew restive under what they regarded as Czech hegemony, and the German-speaking border area of Sudetenland had to be occupied after attempting to break away. These developments had ominous implications for the future integrity of Czechoslovakia.

World War II and Communism

Hitler occupied the Sudetenland in 1938, and the rest of Bohemia and Moravia the following year. The latter remained directly under

Nazi control during the war, but the Slovaks were allowed an 'autonomous' state. At the end of the war Edvard Beneš, the pre-war president, returned to his post and presided over the expulsion of most of the Sudeten Germans (nearly 2.5 million fled or were forced to leave).

The Communist Party quickly infiltrated the organs of government. It also enjoyed great popular support, not least because the 1938 betrayal of Czechoslovakia by Britain and France at Munich was still fresh in people's minds. In the 'Victorious February' of 1948, the Party consolidated its grip without taking up Stalin's offer of military assistance.

The Prague Spring

After 15 years, pressure for reform began to grow, and the hardliners lost

An unofficial sign proclaiming the new Czech Republic in 1993

ground. In 1968, Slovak Alexander Dubček emerged as leader, and pledged to bring in 'socialism with a human face'. The Russians unleashed the Warsaw Pact invasion of August 1968, and Gustáv Husák reimposed orthodoxy, surviving (latterly as president) until the Velvet Revolution of 1989 (*see pp16–17*). Resistance to the invasion was non-violent and symbolic, most dramatically in the case of the student Jan Palach, who committed suicide on Wenceslas Square by setting fire to himself. Some 150,000 people fled the country during this critical period.

1989 and its Consequences

A worsening economy, the more liberal regime of Mikhail Gorbachev in Russia, and the opposition of Charter 77 (formed to monitor human rights) put increasing pressure on the regime, culminating in the 'Velvet Revolution' of November–December 1989, which swept Václav Havel to the presidency. The subsequent break-up of Czechoslovakia into two separate states on 1 January 1993 occurred without a public referendum; Prime Ministers Václav Klaus and Vladimir Meciar did little to halt it on either side.

The Czech Republic (which consists of Bohemia and Moravia) is a pluralist democracy with a government elected by proportional representation. Václav Havel was elected president (by parliament) for a five-year term, although with powers considerably reduced from those that he himself believed he required.

The country has been subjected to a privatisation programme, and has

enormous potential in areas such as tourism (currently to Prague) and foreign direct investment. Its problems are fairly similar to those of other former Soviet satellites.

Unemployment is around 8.5 per cent, though only 4 per cent in Prague. EU entry is one of the current political targets; it is hoped that 2004 will be the entry date. Entry is, however, dependent on legislative reform, improvement of the treatment of minorities, and judicial reform. Today, Prague is an exciting place. Further developments are in the air, and the city glows with increasing affluence (unlike some regions where high unemployment and slow development are still the norm).

Memorial to a modern-day hero: plaque commemorating student Jan Palach

After the crushing of the 'Prague Spring' in 1968, Czechoslovakia sank again under the oppression of Stalinism. Opposition began to surface with the formation of Charter 77. This monitored abuses of human rights in violation of the Helsinki Agreements to which the Communist government was a signatory.

By the mid-1980s, the Czechoslovak Stalinists found themselves increasingly undermined by Mikhail Gorbachev's policy of *perestroika*. Demands for more freedom came from young people, Charter 77, and the Catholic Church.

At the end of 1989 the organisations Civic Forum (in the Czech Republic) and People Against Violence (in Slovakia) were formed in response to police brutality against demonstrators which took place on 17 November.

The following week, vast crowds poured into Wenceslas Square every evening, demanding the resignation of the government. On Friday evening, Dubček addressed the crowds with Václav Havel, the leading personality of Civic Forum.

The Party tried forming a new government with puppet figures, but the tide was running against them. On 10 December, the first cabinet since 1948 with Communists in a minority was announced, together with a promise of multi-party elections in June 1990. Posters immediately appeared with the slogan `HAVEL NA HRAD!' (Havel to the castle!), and demonstrations continued until he was unanimously elected president by the Federal Assembly on 29 December.

The 'Velvet Revolution', as it was dubbed, was not pushing at an open door. Through massive peaceful demonstrations, and the threat of a general strike, it defeated desperate and ruthless men. However, the deciding factor was the refusal of Gorbachev to save the puppet regime maintained by his predecessors. As soon as it was clear that the regime could not summon foreign tanks to save itself, it collapsed like a pack of cards.

Václav Havel – leading the country to democratic stability; facing page: the prison room where Havel was detained

Culture

'Prague always had two faces. She was officially German and unofficially Czech. Or she was officially Czech, but unofficially she had within herself a German city, with its own schools, universities, cinemas, theatres, restaurants, coffee-houses, newspapers. She was officially Austrian, and unofficially anti-Austrian. She was officially Catholic and unofficially anti-Christian . . . .'

WILLY LORENZ
To Bohemia with Love

Religion is a visible aspect of life in Prague

The paradoxical nature of Prague and its people has constantly been reflected in the city's art, architecture, and literature. Religious conflict has been linked to this from earliest times and has shaped the face of the city. Hussite mobs wrecked the interiors of churches, but the Jesuit-led Counter-Reformation, and later, towards the end of the 19th century, Art Nouveau filled Prague with sensual, drama-filled architecture and images.

The pattern of victories and defeats the city has been through has produced a many-layered culture, part of it always submerged. Consequently, Prague has been described as a 'metaphysical madhouse', and a place where 'the absurd is the paradoxical condition of human existence'.

In the 20th century, Czech artists and sculptors began to look to the west. Alfons Mucha, the best known Art Nouveau painter, and the abstract artist František Kupka lived in Paris, while the sculptor František Bílek studied there. Between the wars, the Devětsil (Nine Forces) movement produced Prague's own version of avant-garde art, architecture, and literature.

Detail of doorway, Michna Summer Palace, now the Drovak Museum

Art and Architecture
Prague's rich heritage of architecture begins with the Romanesque buildings

below street level, and three rotunda churches from the 11th and 12th centuries. Gothic architecture dominated the city from the mid-13th century (Cathedral of St Vitus, Týn Church, and St Agnes' Convent). Renaissance style, imported from Italy under the first Habsburgs, is represented above all by the Belvedere, or Summer Palace (1563), built by Ferdinand I.

St Nicholas Church in the Lesser Quarter (Malá Strana)

Mural of scientist on an old building in the Old Town Square

With the Counter-Reformation, Baroque style conquered all. Huge palaces and magnificent churches appeared in the 17th and 18th centuries (St Nicholas in Malá Strana, St Nicholas in Staré Město). This creative energy is clearly manifested in the works of such artists as Karel Škréta and Cosmas Asam. Sculpture was not far behind. Always liberally used to complement architecture, it reached a high point of expressiveness with Matthias Braun, Ferdinand Brokoff, and others.

After a period of historicism, when architecture replicated earlier styles, Prague was swept by the sensuous lines of Art Nouveau at the end of the 19th century (see pp30–31), followed by pioneering experiments with Cubist architecture that are unique to the city (see pp46–7).

Images of Prague

Eloquent images of Prague have been captured by two great Czech photographers – Josef Sudek (1896–1976) and František Drtikol (1878–1961). Sudek is known for his brilliant series of shots (1924) documenting the final phase in seven centuries of building St Vitus' Cathedral. Drtikol's cityscapes range from winter panoramas of ice-clad bridges to the covered stairways and secret alleys of the city.

Even more evocative are the haunting scenes painted by Jakob Schikaneder (1855–1924). *Nocturne in Prague* (1911) is typical: on a chill autumn evening a woman and child hurry into the shadows out of the glare of a gas-light. Schikaneder's is a world of eventide and shadowy figures, of dark buildings splashed with light, and frozen cabmen waiting in snow-covered squares.

Powerful in a different way are the three expressionistic Prague landscapes by Oskar Kokoschka (1886–1980). The turbulent brush-strokes and the bold angle of vision are the most striking in his version of *Charles Bridge and the Hradčany* (1935).

Ukrainian painter Alexandr Onishenko has captured Prague scenes since 1997 in what he terms 'New Impressionism'. He captures visions of the rooftops, trams, and old buildings of Prague. His works, much in demand, are on sale at the Jakubská Galerie (Jakubská, Prague 7).

Music

'Whoever is Czech is a musician' runs a

Dvořák's piano at the museum

Jazz in the Old Town Square

Art gallery, Nerudova, Little Quarter

proverb, and this was certainly the impression given in the Baroque and Romantic eras. Jan Štamic was the court composer in Mannheim; Antonín Rejcha (a great friend of Beethoven) is said to be one of the most underrated composers; and the Italians celebrated Josef Mysliveček as '*il divino Boemo*' (the divine Bohemian), while an appreciative audience in Prague gave Mozart his greatest success with the premiere of his opera *Don Giovanni* (*see p104*).

Detail on building facade

The 19th century produced an outpouring of patriotic romantic music – including such works as *Má Vlast* (*My Country*) by Bedřich Smetana, the *Slavonic Dances* of Antonín Dvořák, or the *Glagolitic Mass* of Leoš Janáček.

Literature and Drama

At the start of the 20th century Prague produced a flowering of writing in German, most famously that of Franz Kafka (*see pp80–81*). Czech writing was chiefly known abroad for the realism of Karel Čapek and Jaroslav Hašek's comic masterpiece *The Good Soldier Švejk*; then came the contemporary wave of writers such as Václav Havel, Milan Kundera, Josef Škvorecký, Bohumil Hrabal, and Ivan Klíma, with works of surreal humour, eroticism, and bleak irony.

The Nobel Prize-winning poet, Jaroslav Seifert, summed up the choice facing Czech writers in the 40 years of Communism: 'When an ordinary person stays silent, it may be a tactical manœuvre. When a writer stays silent, he is lying.'

Today, the new wave of Czech writers includes young authors such as Michal Vieweg (*Bringing up Girls in Bohemia*), whose works are also available in other languages.

Changes

After a decade of political changes, many Czech museums and galleries have now been restored and reopened. However, if you are planning to travel off the beaten track, it's worth double-checking the availability and opening hours of hotels, restaurants, and cultural sites as renovation work is still continuing. Although most telephone numbers in the capital have already become 8-digit, some, particularly those in the regions, remain 6- and 7-digit. If you have difficulty in dialling a number please ring 120 for Prague numbers and 121 for numbers in the Czech Republic.

Interior of the Kafka Café

Impressions

The approaches to Prague, usually through softly rolling hills followed by grey suburbs of panel-built flats, hardly prepare you for the prize at the journey's end. When you finally find yourself in the historic centre, it is as though a curtain has suddenly lifted, revealing a city within a city, jewels of architecture held in a time capsule. The French writer André Breton aptly described this city as 'the magic metropolis of old Europe'.

A complex city captured in a roofscape

Despite its air of being suspended in time, Prague has undergone intensive renovation and reconstruction.

After the Velvet Revolution of 1989, dramatic changes occurred almost overnight. Long-term changes are still

Prague Environs

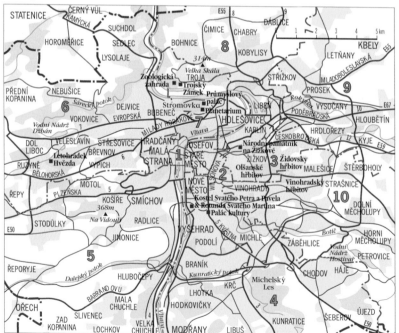

underway but life is stabilising after the flux, uncertainty, and drama of the early 1990s. Visitors may be surprised by the wealth of international brand names, stores such as Tesco and Julius Meinl, and the proliferation of international investors, law firms, and businesses. Many old town houses have been renovated, and a wide range of shops, stores, hypermarkets, and filling stations provide greater choices. Elegant cinema complexes are becoming increasingly commonplace. Decrepit, clattering Trabants and elderly Škodas are being replaced by standard 'Western' cars – indeed, Škoda itself now produces award-winning models such as Felicia, Oktavia, and Fabia.

The backdrop to bustling city life is the cluster of diminutive, historic towns of old Prague. So rich in architectural beauty are these areas, it is little wonder that most Praguers are irrepressible local patriots. Rows of Baroque façades remind one of a film set (and are frequently used as such, as in *Mission Impossible*, *Amadeus*, and *The Lord of the Rings*, to name just a few), while palaces and churches cram the narrow streets of Malá Strana (the Lesser Quarter), and of Hradčany. Here, and in Staré Město (the Old Town), many of these are ancient cobbled alleyways from which cars have long been banned.

In these backwaters, Prague's uniquely ambivalent atmosphere of magic and menace can most powerfully be sensed. An exotic cast of emperors, warlords, religious fanatics, mystical rabbis, and people of many different races have left their mark on the ancient core of the city. The past is a babble of competing voices, the present a turbulent transition. Prague remains, as Egon Erwin Kisch described it, 'the marketplace of sensations'.

When to Go

Prague can be uncomfortably hot in high summer and very cold and raw in winter. The best time to visit the city (and Central Europe generally) is late spring or early autumn. It is not warm before April, and gets rapidly colder after October.

Many Praguers traditionally leave town in summer and head for their *chatas* (chalets) or *chalupas* (cottages) in the country. They now have an added incentive to do so, for the city is full of tourists, particularly in July and August. Although new facilities are being built

The narrow streets of the Old Town (Staré Město) are full of hidden delights

and old ones expanded, it is still preferable to avoid these two months, as well as Whitsun and Easter. Also keep in mind that a number of sights (especially castles and palaces and their gardens) may be closed in winter.

Getting Around

From the visitor's point of view both the topography of Prague and its public transport system are decidedly user-friendly. The main sights are in the compact historic areas of the city (*see pp7-8*) and are ideally visited on foot. The heart of Staré Město is a pedestrian zone, as is most of Wenceslas Square and the whole of the castle area.

Tram

The best way to see the city is by tram. Trams run along both banks of the Vltava, and cross the bridges to traverse Malá Strana as far as the northern approach to the castle. For sightseeing, the No. 22 tram is undoubtedly the best, running from the New Town, across the Vltava to the castle.

Metro

Three lines criss-cross the city. If you take a private room in the suburbs, check that it is close to the metro. Trains run every 4 to 10 minutes at rush hours, every 6 minutes off-peak. A single ticket entitles you to an hour's ride anywhere on the system. Remember that *výstup* means exit and *přestup* indicates an interchange with other lines, and you should have few problems.

Buses

Buses serve outlying areas. You are only

Trams are an attractive alternative to the metro

likely to use them for excursions and a few specific city destinations.

Taxis

Taxis are plentiful, and cheap by western standards. Since the drivers know this, overcharging is common; it is always advisable to check that the meter is turned on (*zapněte taxametr, prosím* is the Czech for requesting this). If you are overcharged, ask for a receipt (*prosím dejte mi potrzení*) and write down the cabbie's number. Avoid picking up taxis from the airport and the Old Town Square as these are ruthlessly expensive. It is cheaper to dial AAA (*02-41014*) and ask to be picked up from wherever you are.

Car

Since the old city is compact and public transport runs up to the edge of its pedestrian zones, there is little point in driving around Prague. Moreover, the local driving style is aggressive and erratic, so street parking is problematic, and being clamped or towed away is the common fate of unwary tourists. It is best to leave your car in a secure garage (*also see p182*).

Pollution in Prague

'Forests dead or dying, rivers dirtied, air unbreathable, soil choked with chemicals.' That is how one publication described the environmental disaster facing the former Czechoslovakia. In addition to acid rain, water pollution, and rivers incapable of supporting fish life, the country's air pollution, as measured by sulphur dioxide emissions per sq km, was the worst in Europe after that of (former) East Germany. The problem in Prague itself is worst in winter because of 'inversion', which traps cold air in the Prague basin, preventing sulphur dioxide from factories, and nitrogen oxide from automobiles, from escaping.

The government has attempted to improve the situation within the constraints of sparse budgets. Brown coal has been replaced as an energy source, wherever possible, to significant effect. This means retaining a nuclear power plant (Temelín) which needs to be brought up to acceptable standards of safety. Neighbouring countries, in particular Austria, and a group of Czechs, fearing another Chernobyl, are lobbying for its closure.

Less controversial is the law requiring all cars sold on the Czech market to have a catalytic converter. In Prague and elsewhere, recycling programmes are very popular, with separate rubbish containers for white or coloured glass, and for paper.

Regular monitoring of air pollution is standard in the media. All this has made some headway, but the massive investment required for the decommissioning or modernisation of polluting factories, and the cleaning up of water supplies, will still take years to materialise.

Manners and Mores

Czechs attach great importance to courtesy: failure to greet your neighbours in the lift or on the stairs, if you are living in a private apartment, could well be taken amiss. Similarly, if you share a café or restaurant table (and you may find you have to), a *dobrý den* (good day) when you sit down, and *a na shledanou* (goodbye) when you leave are *de rigueur*. However, good customer service and friendliness in restaurants and shops is not very common.

Central European housewives are extremely house-proud. Offer to remove your shoes on arrival at a flat. Women have always played a very active role in society, although they continue to juggle full-time jobs with the burden of full domestic responsibilities. Also, don't be surprised to see women bus-drivers or women in top managerial posts.

The Cost of Living

The arrival of democracy and free-market policies exacted a high toll in terms of unemployment (outside Prague) and spiralling prices. Still, Prague will seem reasonable to most visitors: rooms in private houses, substantial meals, and such things as concert tickets may cost as little as half of West European prices.

Prague

'The extraordinary historical treasures of Prague make the city worth the closest observation. It would be a foolish enterprise to write a history of the world without previously visiting this ancient capital.'

CHARLES SEALSFIELD,
German writer (1793–1864)

The cloistered calm of Prague's medieval past

Anežský Klášter (St Agnes' Convent)

The Convent of St Agnes is a particularly fine example of painstakingly restored early Gothic architecture. It was founded at the instigation of Agnes, the sister of Wenceslas 1, in 1234; she preferred the relative freedom of life in a convent to the less attractive proposition of a dynastic marriage.

In 1235 Agnes became the first abbess of the new foundation, which was occupied by the mendicant order of Poor Clares. Some five years later, the Franciscans, male counterparts of the Poor Clares, settled in a monastery next door. The whole complex was sometimes referred to as the 'Bohemian Assisi', after the Italian town where, only a few years earlier, the two orders were founded side by side. There was also a Minorite monastery nearby, remains of which were discovered in the course of 20th-century restoration.

History

Both Agnes and Wenceslas are buried here, as are other members of the Přemyslid dynasty. Notwithstanding the convent's significance as a dynastic burial place (or perhaps because of it), it was vandalised during the Hussite wars

(*see p38*) and the inmates compelled to leave. It was not until 1556 that it was reoccupied – by the Dominicans. The Poor Clares returned in 1627 and remained until 1782.

Emperor Joseph II dissolved the convent in 1782 on the grounds that it served no useful purpose. It was turned into an old people's home and, in the succeeding hundred years, fell into decay. Some parts became a slum, while others were a rabbit warren of craftsmen's studios. In the 1890s, a patriotic fund was inaugurated to clean up the area and restore the buildings.

It was in 1989, on the eve of the Velvet Revolution, shortly before Pope John Paul II's historic visit to Prague, that the first abbess of the Order of the Poor Charles was canonised.

The Buildings

The cloister, dating to about 1260, is an open arcade around a square courtyard. It has a heavy vaulted ceiling characteristic of early Gothic. To the east, reached through a passage, is the most impressive of the surviving buildings, the Kostel Sv Salvátora (Church of the Holy Saviour). An interesting feature of this French-influenced Gothic church is the relief portraits on the capitals of the arched entrance, apparently those of the kings and queens of the Přemyslid dynasty. The head over the salvation altar is thought by scholars to be that of St Agnes herself, watching over the nearby entrance to the royal crypt. One of the loveliest areas of the church is that of the choir.

South of the Church of the Holy Saviour is the Kostel Sv František (Church of St Francis), dating to about 1240, a somewhat severe edifice built according to the puritanical architectural norms laid down by the Minorites. King Wenceslas I is buried in this church, which has only recently reacquired a roof. It is now used for lectures and frequent concerts.

The convent also houses the Czech National Gallery's collections (*see pp108–9*) and a range of temporary exhibitions.

U milosrdných 17. Staré Město, Praha I. Tel: (02) 2187 9216. Open: Tue–Sun 10am–6pm. Admission charge. Trams: 5, 14, & 26 to Revolucní.

The beautifully restored Gothic Convent of St Agnes

Art Nouveau Architecture

Art Nouveau, a term first used in Paris in 1895, liberated architecture and the fine arts from rigid formalism and quotation. The natural world was its touchstone; it luxuriated in decorative flowing lines with floral patterns and exotic ornament.

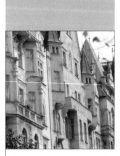
The grandeur of Pařížska Street

When Art Nouveau arrived in Prague, much of central European architecture seemed frozen in time. Those who gave the big commissions – principally the State and the Church – expected architects to adhere to the styles of the past. After a while, this so-called 'historicism' began to degenerate into a sterile and pompous reproduction of motifs from pattern books. Art Nouveau not only represented a new aesthetic approach, but also took advantage of advances in construction technology, using materials such as cast iron, steel and glass.

Prague contains some of the most fascinating Art Nouveau works in the world, though here they are usually labelled 'modern style' or *secesní* after the Viennese Secession movement. One of the most successful proponents of the new style in Paris was the Czech, Alfons Mucha (1860–1939), renowned for his enduringly popular posters. You can see some of his work in the Mayor's Hall, which is the highlight of a visit to the beautifully renovated Obecní dům (the Muncipal House on Náměstí Republiky, *see pp120–21*), completed in 1911 and, perhaps, the most ambitious and visually stunning of Prague's Secessionist buildings.

Art Nouveau window in St Vitus' Cathedral

Evropa Hotel (Europa Hotel)
This sadly shabby but highly ornate hotel is essential viewing for anyone nostalgic about a world that died in 1914. It was built in 1903–5 by Alois Dryák and Bedřich Bendelamayer. *25 Václavské náměstí. Tel: (02) 2422 8117/2422 4544. Café open: 7am–11pm. Metro: to Muzeum or Můstek.*

Hanavský Pavilón (Hanava Pavilion)
Built for the Paris World Exhibition of

1878, the pavilion is a historicist folly. The use of cast iron in the construction gives it an Art Nouveau flavour. There is an expensive but good restaurant here. *Letenské sady. Tel: (02) 3332 3641. Open: daily noon–1am. Terrace café open: summer, sunrise–sunset. Trams: 12 & 17 to Čechůvg, then climb the steps up to the park.*

Hlavní Nádraží (Central Railway Station)
One of the most monumental of Prague's Art Nouveau buildings, the façade and concourse for the station were designed by Josef Fanta in 1909. Today, it is in a poor state of repair. *Wilsonova. Metro: (line C) to Hlavní nádraží.*

Peterkův Dům (Peterka House)
A rather restrained example of Art Nouveau by Jan Kotěra, a pupil of the great Viennese Secessionist architect, Otto Wagner. *12 Václavské náměstí. Not open to the public. Metro: to Muzeum or Můstek.*

Pojišťovna Praha (Prague Savings Bank) and Topičův Dům (State Publishing House)
The buildings, Nos 7 and 9 respectively, are neighbours on Národní. Note the lavish mosaic lettering above the windows, advertising the bank's various services, and the ceramic reliefs in the gable of the Topič publishing house. Both houses were designed by Oswald Polívka and built between 1907 and 1908 (*see pp44–5*). *7 & 9 Národní. Not open to the public. Trams: 6, 9, 18, & 22 to Národní divadlo.*

Josef Fanta's Central Station

Průmyslový Palác (Industrial Palace)
Bedřich Münzberger's huge steel and glass construction, built for the Bohemia Jubilee Exhibition of 1891, is the first Prague building that recognisably embodies the spirit of Art Nouveau. It still has Neo-Baroque features, but the materials used were innovative. *Praha 7, Výstaviště. Open: May–Sep 10am–5.30pm. Free admission except evenings. Metro: to Nádraží Holešovice. Trams: 5, 12, & 17 to Výstaviště.*

Those hungry for more can pick up an interesting, beautifully illustrated booklet entitled *Art Nouveau in Prague* by Petr Balajka, available at any bookshop.

The Vltava (Moldau to the Germans) dominates Prague as few other rivers dominate a capital city. In the past, whole sections of the population used to live off it, though it had less appealing roles as well: thieves and adulterers were suspended in its icy waters in wicker baskets from the Charles Bridge; John of Nepomuk, the 14th-century canon who supported his archbishop against King Wenceslas IV, was thrown into it and drowned.

Nowadays, the once wild river that regularly used to burst its banks has been tamed by six dams along its 430-km course. In front of Charles Bridge it is a mere pond, with people splashing about in rowing boats and pedaloes. Unfortunately, the river remains unhealthy. Vltava fish featured on Prague menus have to be caught upstream from where the dangerously polluted Berounka flows into the main river – a sad decline from the Middle Ages, when the city's apprentices complained that they were fed salmon every day.

The romantic image of the river is preserved in the city's memorials to it. For instance, the Vltava water nymph (known affectionately as 'Terezka') may be seen on the wall of the Clam-Gallas Palace's gardens on Mariánské náměstí. The most beloved monument is on the

northern tip of the Dětský ostrov (the Children's Island). From here, wreaths for the river's many victims are thrown into the water in November. On All Souls' Day, a boat decked with black flags sets out on the dark waters as the city commemorates its dead.

Glimpses of the Vltava and its surroundings – a river for all seasons and the soul of the city

Belvedér

It was between 1538 and 1563 that the Královská zahrada (Royal Gardens, *see p51*) and a surpassingly elegant 'Lustschloss' (country seat) took shape on a patch of land a little to the northeast of Hradčany. This was the summer palace built by Ferdinand I for his wife, Anna Jagiello; the design and its garden setting show a strong Italian influence.

The original architect of the Belvedere (as the palace is known), Paolo della Stella, was responsible for the slim-columned arcade with its mythological reliefs that gives the palace its southern look, and reminds one that it was a retreat for the court in the warm months. Bonifaz Wohlmut, the court architect who also built the Ball Game Court in the gardens, completed the ambitious project between 1552 and 1569. His design of the copper roof is unusual, like the hull of an upturned ship, now a mellow green through oxidisation. Rudolf II, Ferdinand's grandson, was particularly fond of the Belvedere, and encouraged his Danish astronomer, Tycho Brahe, to set up an observatory on the terrace. After Brahe's death, Johannes Kepler, his assistant, succeeded him as imperial mathematician, and his *Laws of Planetary Motion,* published in 1609, were based on work done at the Belvedere.

The Swedes plundered the palace in 1648, and Joseph II turned it into a military laboratory. A proper restoration was undertaken only in the mid-19th century, when a cycle of historical painting dealing with the leitmotifs of

Spectacular ceiling frescoes in the Břevnov Monastery

Bohemian history was added to the first-floor rooms.

Hradčany, Praha 1. Open: May–Sep, Tue–Sun 10am–6pm. Admission charge. Trams: 22 & 23 to Belvedere.

Bývalý Benediktinský Klášter (Břevnov Monastery)

Legend has it that Duke Boleslav II and Bishop Adalbert of Prague were joint founders of Břevnov Monastery in 993, which would make it the oldest monastery in Bohemia. The site of the monastery was supposedly revealed to them in a dream. Such cooperation would be remarkable, if true, in that it pre-dates the massacre of Adalbert's (Slavník) family by their rivals for power, Boleslav's (Přemyslid) family, by only two years.

Apart from the crypt, there are hardly any Romanesque or Gothic architectural remains. The church, once dedicated to St Adalbert, was probably rededicated to St Margaret in the second half of the 14th century after her remains were transferred here in the 13th century. What we see today is the result of a complete rebuilding in Baroque style, between 1708 and 1745, by Christoph and Karl Dientzenhofer.

Dientzenhofer and his son, Kilián Ignác, turned Břevnov into one of the glories of Bohemian Baroque. The Kostel Sv Markéta (St Margaret's Church) is a masterwork of visionary architecture. Its marching series of diagonally protruding pillars support oval ceiling spaces covered with frescoes.

The tightly focused effect recalls Dientzenhofer's Church of St Nicholas in Malá Strana.

Other highlights include the frescoes in the Prelates' Hall by Cosmas Asam. The Library also has fine allegorical frescoes by Felix Scheffler, and the Refectory is notable for Bernhard Spinetti's stucco and Jan Kovář's manneristic painting on the ceiling.

The monastery has undergone complete restoration in recent years. The Communists had turned it into an archive, but the Benedictines are now back at Břevnov.

Open for tours: 1 Apr–8 Oct, Sat 9am, 10.30am, 1pm, 2.30pm, & 4pm, Sun 10.30am, 1pm, 2.30pm, & 4pm; 9 Oct-31 Mar, Sat–Sun 8am & 2pm. Trams: 8 & 22, alighting at Břevnovský Klášter.

The Belvedere Summer Palace, built by Ferdinand I, the first Habsburg king of Bohemia

Cemeteries

Malostranský Hřbitov
(Lesser Quarter Cemetery)
Opened in 1680 for plague victims, the graveyard continued in use until 1884.
Prague 5. Trams: 4, 7, & 9 to Plzeňská ulice, Bertramka.

Olšanské Hřbitov
(Olšany Cemetery)
One of the biggest cemeteries of Central Europe, with over 100,000 graves. Student Jan Palach is buried here.
Prague 3, Vinohradská třída.
Trams: 10, 11, 16, & 26. Metro: Flora.

Starý Židovský Hřbitov
(Old Jewish Cemetery)
See pp76–7.

Vinohradský Hřbitov
(Vinohrady Cemetery)
Celebrated artists, actors, singers, and writers are buried here, most notably the journalist Egon Erwin Kisch.
Prague 10, Vinohradská třída.
Trams: 11 & 26.

Vyšehradský Hřbitov
(Vyšehrad Cemetery)
Celebrities buried here include the novelists Karel Čapek and Jan Neruda, and composers Antonín Dvořák and Bedřich Smetana.
Prague 2, Vyšehrad. Metro: Vyšehrad.

Židovský Hřbitov
(Jewish Cemetery)
Franz Kafka's grave is in section 21, row 14, at No. 33.
Trams 11, 16, & 26. Metro: Želivského.

Central Prague

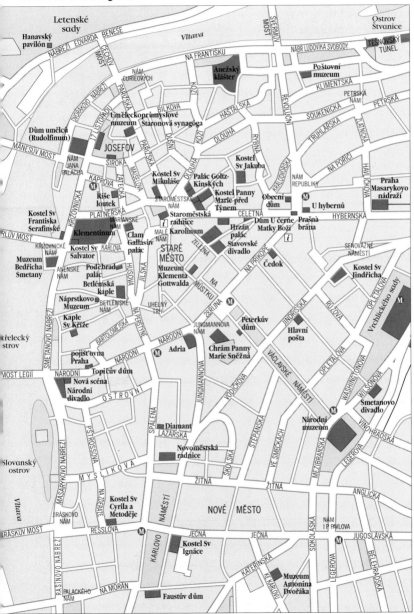

Letenské sady

Hanavský pavilón

Vltava

Ostrov Štvanice

TĚSNOVSKÝ TUNEL

NÁBŘEŽÍ EDVARDA BENEŠE

NA FRANTIŠKU

NÁBŘ LUDVÍKA SVOBODY

DVOŘÁKOVO NÁBŘEŽÍ

ČECHŮV MOST

ŠVERMŮV MOST

NÁM. CURIEOVYCH

Anežský klášter

Poštovní muzeum

KLIMENTSKÁ

PETRSKÁ NÁM

PETRSKÁ

17 LISTOPADU

PAŘÍŽSKÁ

IZÓ

BILKOVA

HAŠTALSKÁ

REVOLUČNÍ

SOUKENICKÁ

TRUHLÁŘSKÁ

LÁTKOVÁ

Dům umělců (Rudolfinum)

Uměleckoprůmyslové muzeum Staronová synagóga

DUŠNÍ

KOZÍ

DLOUHÁ

RYBNÁ

NA POŘÍČÍ

HAVLÍČKOVA

MÁNESŮV MOST

JOSEFOV

NÁM JANA PALACHA

ŠIROKÁ

PAŘÍŽSKÁ

Kostel Sv Jakuba

KRÁLODVORSKÁ

NÁM REPUBLIKY

Praha Masarykovo nádraží

KŘIŽOVNICKÁ

KAPROVA

ZÁTECKÁ

MASLOVA

Kostel Sv Mikuláše

DLOUHÁ

Palác Goltz-Kinských

Kostel Panny Marie před Týnem

Obecní dům

U hybernů

Říše loutek

STAROMĚSTSKÉ NÁM

CELETNÁ

HYBERNSKÁ

Kostel Sv Františka Serafinského

PLATNÉŘSKÁ

MARIÁNSKÉ NÁM

Staroměstská radnice

Dům U černé Matky Boží

Prašná brána

KARLŮV MOST

Klementinum

Clam Gallasův palác

MALÉ NÁM

Karolinum

Hrzán palác

SENOVÁŽNÉ NÁMĚSTÍ

KŘIŽOVNICKÉ NÁM

KARLOVA

ŽELEZNÁ

Stavovské divadlo

Muzeum Bedřicha Smetany

Kostel Sv Salvator

ANENSKÉ NÁM

HUSOVA

JILSKÁ

STARÉ MĚSTO

NA PŘÍKOPĚ

Čedok

Kostel Sv Jindřicha

Poděbrad palác

Muzeum Klementa Gottwalda

NA MŮSTKU

Náprstkovo Muzeum

BETLÉMSKÉ NÁM

UHELNÝ TRH

JINDŘIŠSKÁ

RŮŽOVÁ

Vrchlického sady

Betlémská kaple

NA PERŠTÝNĚ

ZBRUNA

Peterkův dům

Hlavní pošta

OPLETALOVA

Kaple Sv Kříže

BARTOLOMĚJSKÁ

JUNGMANNOVA NÁM

střelecký ostrov

SMETANOVO NÁBŘEŽÍ

pojišťovna Praha

NÁRODNÍ

Adria

Chrám Panny Marie Sněžná

VÁCLAVSKÉ NÁMĚSTÍ

WASHINGTONOVA

WILSONOVA

MOST LEGIÍ

NÁRODNÍ

Topičův dům

OPLETALOVA

Smetanovo divadlo

Nová scéna

Národní divadlo

OSTROVNÍ

JUNGMANNOVA

VODIČKOVA

ŠTĚPÁNSKÁ

VE SMEČKÁCH

MEZIBRANSKÁ

VINOHRADSKÁ

PŠTROSSOVA

SPÁLENÁ

Diamant

LAZARSKÁ

Národní muzeum

LEGEROVA

Slovanský ostrov

MASARYKOVO NÁBŘEŽÍ

MYSLÍKOVA

NA ZDERAZE

Novoměstská radnice

ŠKOLSKÁ

ŽITNÁ

ŽITNÁ

ANGLICKÁ

Vltava

JIRÁSKOVO NÁM

RESSLOVA

Kostel Sv Cyrila a Metoděje

NÁMĚSTÍ

NOVÉ MĚSTO

SOKOLSKÁ

NÁM I P PAVLOVA

JUGOSLÁVSKÁ

JIRÁSKŮV MOST

KARLOVO

JEČNÁ

JEČNÁ

LEGEROVA

BĚLEHRADSKÁ

RAŠÍNOVO NÁBŘEŽÍ

Kostel Sv Ignáce

KATEŘINSKÁ

KE KARLOVU

PALACKÉHO NÁM

NA MORÁŇ

Faustův dům

Muzeum Antonína Dvořáka

Churches

Prague boasts an astonishing wealth of ecclesiastical architecture. By the end of the 14th century there were 26 convents and monasteries in the city; scores of churches were built in the Middle Ages, the Baroque period, and the 19th century. This list of churches includes ones not covered under Hradčany, Staroměstské náměstí, and Malostranské náměstí. It excludes churches attached to convents where the latter have their own entries. Where access is limited, this has been noted.

Betlémská Kaple (Bethlehem Chapel)

The present building is a modern replica of the Gothic trapezoidal chapel founded in 1391. It was rebuilt between 1536 and 1539, acquired by the Jesuits in 1661, and virtually demolished in 1786. The 14th-century church authorities, who had agreed to the construction of a 'chapel', were faced with a building that could accommodate 3,000, was a focus of church reform, and a lasting spiritual centre of Hussitism – Jan Hus himself preached at the chapel.

In the adjoining preacher's house are exhibits relating to the Hussites, and a reconstruction of

a 15th-century domestic interior (*see pp102–3*). *Staré Město. Betlémské náměstí. Open: daily, Apr–Oct 9am–6pm; Nov–Mar 9am–5pm. Metro: Můstek or Národní třída.*

Jan Hus presides over Old Town Square

Kostel Svatého Cyrila a Metodéje (Church of St Cyril and Methodius)

This somewhat forbidding church, completed by Kilián Dientzenhofer in 1740, was originally dedicated to St Charles Borromeo. When the Czech Orthodox Church took it over in 1935, it was rededicated to St Cyril and St Methodius. The crypt contains memorials of resistance fighters who took refuge there after assassinating the Nazi governor of Bohemia in 1942.

Nové Město, Resslova ulice. Admission at times other than for mass is difficult.
Metro: Karlovo náměstí.

Kostel Svatého Františka Serafinského (Church of St Francis Seraphicus)

The richly decorated church (1689) is notable for its imposing cupola with VL Reiner's fresco of *The Last Judgement* (1722), and for its walls clad in Bohemian marble.

Staré Město, Křížovnické náměstí.
Trams: 17 & 18.
Metro: Staroměstská.

Kostel Svatého Jakuba (Church of St James)

St James's is a Baroque reconstruction of an earlier Gothic building (*see p129*). The long, glittering interior is furnished with 21 elegantly carved altars, above which are open galleries and a magnificent series of frescoes (*The Life of the Virgin* and *The Adoration of the Trinity* by Franz Guido Voget). The altarpiece is Václav Reiner's version of *The Martyrdom of St James*. The impressive marble and sandstone tomb in the left-hand nave is of Count Vratislav of Mitrovic, a Bohemian Chancellor.

Staré Město, Malá Štupartská.
Metro: Náměstí Republiky or Můstek.

St James's Church in the Old Town, one of the loveliest churches in Prague

Kostel Svatého Jana Nepomuckého Na Skalce (Church of St John Nepomuk on the Rock)

This is one of the architect Kilián Ignác Dientzenhofer's masterworks. A double flight of balustraded steps sweeps up to the twin-towered late-Baroque façade (1739). Inside, the ceiling fresco of *The Ascension of St John Nepomuk* by Karel Kovář is of exceptional quality, as is Jan Brokoff's altar statue of the saint, a model for the version later placed on Charles Bridge.

Nové Město, Vyšehradská třída.
Admission at times other than for mass is difficult.
Trams: 4, 14, 16, 18, & 24 to Karlovo náměstí.
Metro: to Karlovo naměsti.

Kostel Nanebevzetí Panny Marie a Karla Velikého (Church of the Assumption of Our Lady and Charlemagne)

Charles IV founded the monastery (part of the former Augustinian monastery known as Karlov) in 1350, and stipulated that the design for the church should follow Charlemagne's Imperial Chapel at Aachen, but some of the building's finest parts (such as the remarkable star vaulting) were completed by Bonifaz Wohlmut only in the 16th century. The pilgrims' steps on the south side are a Baroque addition on the model of the Scala Santa in Rome. Don't miss the side galleries with theatrical sculptures by JJ Schlansovsk (*The Annunciation* and *Christ Before Pilate*).

Nové Město, Ke Karlovu.
Metro: IP Pavlova.

Exploring the frescoes at the Church of St John Nepomuk on the Rock

Chrám Panny Marie Sněžná (Church of Our Lady of the Snows)

This building was planned as a Coronation Cathedral by Charles IV, but construction had got no further than the lofty choir before being interrupted by the Hussite rebellion. Jan Želivský, the radical reformer, was buried here after his execution in 1421. The angry demonstration that ended with the first defenestration of Prague began in Our Lady of the Snows on 30 July 1419.

Nové Město, Jungmannova náměstí.
Metro station: Můstek.

Kostel Panny Marie Vítizné (Church of St Mary the Victorious)

This was Prague's first Baroque church (1613), ironically commissioned by Lutherans – since the Baroque style is associated with militant Catholicism. The Carmelites later rebuilt it. Inside is the *Bambino di Praga*, a Spanish wax model of the infant Jesus, with supposed

miraculous powers. It is an object of great Catholic veneration, and wears a spectacular array of clothing which is changed according to religious festivals.
Malá Strana, Karmelitská ulice.
Trams: 12 & 22 to Hellichova.

Kostel Nejsvětějšiho Srdce Páne (Church of the Sacred Heart)

Anyone with an interest in architecture should visit this, a stunning example of Josip Plečnik's work, built in 1933 under the influence of the Viennese school of Otto Wagner. At the east end is a massive pedimental tower with a gigantic clock set in it like a rose window – a foretaste of contemporary Post-Modernism. The interior, though functionalist, has nobility and grace. Look for the stylised wooden statues of Bohemian saints by D Pesan, who also sculpted the monumental gilded Christ.
Prague 3, Náměstí Jiřího z Poděbrad.
Metro station on the square.

Kostel Svatého Tomáše (Church of St Thomas)

Kilián Ignác Dientzenhofer remodelled this church in Baroque style in 1731. Traces can be seen of earlier rebuildings of the Romanesque original in Gothic and Renaissance style. Ceiling frescoes by Václav Reiner depict the *Life of St Augustine* (in the cupola) and the *Legend of St Thomas*. Karel Škréta, one of the greatest of Prague's early Baroque painters, did several of the altarpieces. Over the high altar are copies of *The Martyrdom of St Thomas* and *St Augustine,* commissioned for the church from Rubens (the originals are in the National Gallery).

Buried in the cloister is an English humanist poetess at the court of Rudolf II, Elizabeth Jane Weston (or 'Vestonia' under her Latin *nom de plume*).
Mála Strana, Letenská ulice.
Trams: 12 & 22 to Malostranské náměstí.
Metro: Malostranská.

The Church of the Sacred Heart in Vinohrady is a modernist masterpiece

Walk: Churches of Nové Město

This walk gives a taste of the rich heritage left by Prague's two great waves of Gothic and Baroque church building in the Nové Město (New Town).

Allow 2 hours.

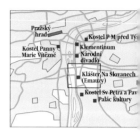

Begin at the metro station on Karlovo náměstí (line B), take the Karlovo náměstí exit, and walk downhill along Resslova.

1 Kostel Svatého Cyrila a Metodéje

On your right is the Church of St Cyril and St Methodius, the Czech Orthodox cathedral (*see p39*). A plaque on the wall reminds you that it was here that the Free Czech paratroopers who assassinated the Nazi governor of Bohemia, Richard Heydrich, made their last stand on 18 June 1942 (*see p98 &*

p142). Across the street is Kostel Svatého Václava (St Wenceslas Church). The Hussite congregation, which now owns St Wenceslas, is the modern successor to the warring Hussites suppressed by the Counter-Reformation.

Walk back up Resslova, turn right into Václavská, and go as far as Na Moráni. Turn left up to the junction with Vyšehradská, then right.

2 Faustův Dům

On the corner with U nemocnice is the Baroque Faustův dům ('Faust

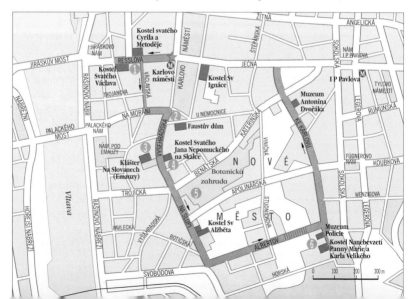

House'), where the opening scene of the Czech version of the Faust legend takes place. Rudolf II's English alchemist, Edward Kelley, is supposed to have lived in an earlier Renaissance house on this site.
Walk straight on.

3 Klášter Na Slovanech
The Emmaus Monastery is one of the few buildings in Prague to suffer bomb damage in the war. The most dramatic aspects of its restoration are the two reinforced concrete sail-like spires.
Continue further along on the left.

4 Kostel Svatého Jana Nepomuckého Na Skalce
The Church of St John Nepomuk on the Rock (*see p40*) is one of Kilián Dientzenhofer's loveliest Baroque creations. It is difficult to access (although you may be able to do so during mass), but even from the outside you can admire how the architect has cunningly turned to advantage the steep and narrow site on which this elegant little church is perched.
As Vyšehradská merges into Na slupi, you can turn off left into the Botanical Garden.

5 Botanická Zahrada
The glasshouse of exotic flora is worth the small entrance charge, and you can lose yourself happily for half an hour among the dense shrubbery and meandering paths (*see p48*).
Continue along and turn left up Albertov. Climb the steps at the end on to Ke Karlovu.

Lily-pads at the Botanická Zahrada

6 Kostel Nanebevzetí Panny Marie a Karla Velikého
On the right is the 14th-century Church of the Assumption of Our Lady and Charlemagne, inspired by Charlemagne's burial chapel at Aachen. The stellar vaulting is built without central supports, which caused the architect to be accused of being devilish – remarkable features include 'holy steps' (which pilgrims had to ascend on their knees), theatrical Baroque balcony scenes, and a Bethlehem grotto in the crypt.
  The Muzeum Policie (Police Museum) is adjacent to the church. You return along Ke Karlovu, passing the Muzeum Antonína Dvořáka (Antonín Dvořák Museum – Vila Amerika, (*see p105*) on the way.
Trams to the centre leave from Ječná at the far end of the street.

Walk: Nové Město

'New' is a decidedly relative term in Prague: the original Nové Město was founded by Charles IV as long ago as 1348. The king created this new quarter of the city to link Staré Město with the fortress of Vyšehrad. In the late 19th century the area was largely reconstituted, and a slum was transformed into streets and squares exuding middle-class respectability and self-confidence.

Allow 1 hour.

Begin at Národní divadlo (trams 6, 9, 18, 22, & 23) and walk east along Národní.

1 Národní Divadlo

On your right is Kostel Svaté Voršily (the Ursuline Church), part of a convent, which is occasionally open, so that one can drop in to admire the Baroque frescoes. On the outside is a striking statue of St John of Nepomuk; according to the legend, he was thrown into the Danube on 20 March 1393, on the orders of Wenceslas IV, for refusing to reveal the secrets of the Queen's confession.

Across the street are two exceptionally fine examples of Art Nouveau architecture, the Pojišťovna Praha (Prague Savings Bank) at No. 7 and the Topičův dům (Topič publishing house) at No. 9. A feature of the bank is the

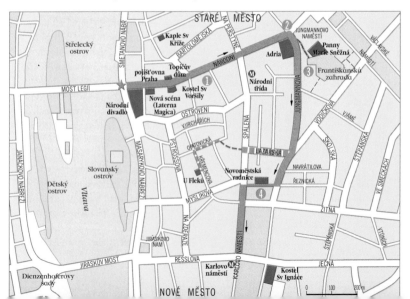

mosaic slogans above the windows advertising life insurance, loans, pensions, and 'dowries'.

Further up the street on the right (No. 16), a small shrine under an arcade commemorates the victims of police brutality on 17 November 1989 that triggered the 'Velvet Revolution'. Nearby is the British Council building, retaining a 'Constructivist' façade from the 1930s (you can also pop in to read its journals, magazines, and newspapers in the ground-floor atrium).

In Prague even the New Town Hall (scene of the first defenestration) is medieval

2 Jungmannovo Náměstí

At the end of Národní is Jungmannovo náměstí, named after a leading figure of the 19th-century Czech literary revival, whose statue dominates the square. To the south is the Cubist Adria Palace, with a pleasant terrace café. The basement contains a theatre where Civic Forum used to meet after 17 November 1989.

On the eastern edge of the square is the celebrated Cubist lamp post, which stands close to the entrance to Chrám Panny Marie Sněžná (Church of Our Lady of the Snows, *see pp40–41*). Charles IV planned this as a great coronation church, but the money ran out when only the chancel was complete. The soaring Baroque high altar is impressive, but the whole has a rather gloomy atmosphere.

Turn left out of the church.

3 Františkánská Zahrada

You soon come to the entrance to the Františkánská Zahrada (Franciscan Gardens) to the southeast, part of the Franciscan monastery that ranges along their northwest wall. The gardens are a pleasant place to eat a picnic lunch picked up from one of the purveyors on Václavské náměstí (Wenceslas Square) or one of the many covered passages only a couple of minutes from here.

Returning to Jungmannovo náměstí, bear left down Jungmannova. Just beyond the junction with Vodičkova, Karlovo náměstí begins. On the way you can detour to U Fleků, where a famous black beer is brewed on the premises (see pp172–3). Turn right into Lazarská, go through a passageway at Spálená 15 into Opatovická, then turn left for Křemencova 11. The beer hall is on your right. Retrace your steps to the end of Lazarská, then turn right into Vodičkova.

4 Novoměstská Radnice

On your right is the ancient-looking Novoměstská radnice (New Town Hall). The tower, entrance hall, and cellars are genuinely medieval. The first defenestration of Prague took place here in 1419 when Hussites threw Catholic councillors out of the windows for refusing to release reformist prisoners.

Trams back to the centre may be picked up on Ječná, which traverses Karlovo náměstí.

Cubist Architecture

In 1910, the appropriately named Czech painter, Bohumil Kubišta, wrote excitedly home from Paris informing his colleagues that Picasso and Braque were the artists of the future. There followed a vogue in Prague for Cubist painting and Cubist design in the applied arts and architecture. In 1911, the influential Skupina výtvarných umělců (Group of Fine Artists) was established, with its own journal, and overnight (or so it seemed) Cubist houses appeared, filled with Cubist furniture and Cubist household articles.

The rapid acceptance of Cubism (and Modernism generally) demonstrated the Czech determination to overcome their historical status as a provincial backwater. Cubism was attractive to artists and intellectuals who thought of Czech culture as part of the European mainstream; yet it was natural that there should be something characteristically 'Czech' about the local variants of Modernism. Cubist buildings by Josef Gočár (1880–1948), Josef Chochol (1880–1956), and Pavel Janák (1882–1956) recall Bohemian Baroque in their harmonious proportions and geometrical play of surfaces. Indeed, one of the earliest Cubist buildings by Goãár was accepted by the general public because it harmonised with its Baroque

---

BUILDINGS

Josef Gočár: Dům U Černé Matky Boží (Black Madonna House), Celetná ulice 19. Metro: Náměstí Republiky. Bank Legií, Na poříčí 24. Metro: Náměstí Republiky.

Josef Chochol: Neklanova ulice 30 and Libušina ulice 3. Trams: 7, 18, & 24 to Na slupi. Rašínovo nábřeží 6–10. Trams: 3, 7, & 17 to Výtoň.

Otakar Novotný: Ulice Elišky Krásnohorské 123. Trams: 17 & 18 to Pravnická fakulta.

Pavel Janák: Adria Palace, Jungmannova 31. Metro: Národní třída or Můstek.

Emil Králíček: Diamond House, Spálená ulice 4. Metro: Národní třída.

---

neighbours on Celetná ulice.

After the founding of the Czechoslovak Republic, Cubism developed into a 'National Style' or 'Rondocubism', intended as an expression of 'Slav' identity, but with both Cubist and traditional features. The façade of Janák's Rondocubist Adria Palace, which mixes all three elements, brings to mind a futuristic Italian Renaissance palace.

Although abstract form is central in Cubism, the play of geometrical surfaces in Prague's Cubist buildings provides a sensuality far removed from the arid anonymity of much modern architecture. Some people are impressed by their boldness, others find them sinister; either way, these buildings are impossible to ignore.

In 1912 Josef Gočár built the Dům U Černé Matky Boží (Black Madonna House) on Celetná ulice. It was so-called because a Baroque statue of the Madonna from the previous house on the site was retained on the façade. There are four storeys, the first three of which consist almost entirely of windows, so that the building seems to be all eyes and no face. Josef Chochol built more Cubist houses than any of his colleagues, whose designs often remained on paper. On Neklanova ulice in Vyšehrad is perhaps his most famous one, an apartment block with wedge-shaped forms on the façade and an overhanging cornice. Chochol designed the nearby Kovařovičova Villa on Libušina ulice, where even the garden and railings are Cubist. On Rašínovo nábřeží is his three-family house (Rodinnˇ trojdům), described as being 'like a classical palace', perhaps because of its relief-covered pediment.

On Ulice Elišky Krásnohorské is Otakar Novotný's Rondocubist building, one of the first to have a façade enlivened by colour contrasts. The best known Rondocubist work is Pavel Janák's Adria Palace. Another vivid example is the Bank Legií by Gočár on Na poříčí (now the Ministry for Industry) – with a patriotic frieze by Otto Gutfreund on the wall. Emil Králíček's Diamant (Diamond House – 1912) on Spálená ulice offers a coruscating display of variations on the diamond form – not beautiful, but undeniably arresting.

Janák's Rondocubist Adria Palace

Gardens and Parks

Garden culture has a long tradition in Prague and reached its apotheosis in the Baroque period. By the mid-18th century, gardens bejewelled the north slope of Petřín Hill, the slopes beneath Strahov, and the southern reaches of Hradčany. In the 19th and 20th centuries, many of the city's most attractive green spaces became municipal parks.

Plants for sale in the Botanical Garden (Botanická Zahrada)

Botanická Zahrada (Botanical Garden)

Prague boasted of a botanical garden even in the 14th century. Situated where the main Post Office is now, it was run by a Florentine apothecary. The present garden is charming though a bit run-down (*see p43*).
Prague 2, Na slupi 16. Open: daily 10am–7pm. Trams: 18 & 24 to Na slupi. A second botanical garden is located in Troja at Nádvorní 134. Open: daily 9am–6pm.

Chotkovy Sady (Chotek Park)

Founded by Count Chotek in 1833 as the city's first public park, Chotek Park contains a bizarre monument to the poet Julius Zeyer (1844–1901).
Trams: 18 & 22 to Chotkovy sady.

Kinských Zahrada (Kinsky Gardens)

Prince Kinsky employed Franz Höhnel to lay out this park as an English landscape garden in 1825. It passed to the municipality in 1901. Kinsky Gardens contain a Neo-Classical villa, once used by Crown Prince Rudolf and the Archduke Franz Ferdinand. Other curiosities are an 18th-century wooden church transported from a village in the Carpatho-Ukraine in 1929, and a picturesque little campanile from Moravia.
Entrance on náměstí Kinských or from Petřín through the medieval 'Hunger Wall'. Trams 6, 9, or 23 & 22 to Újezd.

Královská Zahrada (The Royal Gardens)

Laid out in 1534, these gardens formed the first Italian Renaissance gardens of Central Europe. A report of 1650 marvels at the varied varieties of fruit, pomegranates, figs, lemons, and limes grown here, and at the tigers, lions, lynxes, and bears that were kept in the menagerie.

It was here that the botanist Mathioli cultivated the first European tulips in the 16th century. At the north end of the gardens is the Belvedere (*see p34*), and on the east side you will pass the sgraffitoed Ball Game Court designed by Bonifaz Wohlmut, which was later used as a ballroom.
Open: Apr–Sep Tue–Sun 10am–6pm. Closed: Mon. Admission charge. Tram: 22 to Pražský hrad.

Palace Gardens below Prague Castle

Three gardens in Malá Strana were restored in the 1950s, and since 1989 increasing sections of the ravishing terraces below the castle have been opened to the public. The entrance is via the Kolowrat-Černín Palace, whose garden is laid out with Rococo stairways, terraces, fountains, and ornamental pools.

Valdštejnská 12. Currently the Malá Palffyho and Ledeburská gardens are open 10am–6pm. Metro: Malostranská.

Vojanovy Sady (Vojan Park)

Tucked away in the lower part of Malá Strana is Vojan Park, former convent gardens. To the left of the entrance is a statue of St John Nepomuk standing on a fish. Another curiosity is St Elias Chapel, which is an imitation stalactite cave, that has ceiling frescoes of episodes in the saint's life.

Entrance from U Lužického semináře. Metro: Malostranská.

Vrtbovská Zahrada (Vrtba Gardens)

The Vrtba, among the finest of Prague's Baroque terraced gardens, are noted for Matthias Braun's statuary: an Atlas near the entrance, and Ceres and Bacchus at the lower end.

Karmelitská ulice 26. Open 10am–6pm, longer in summer. Trams 12, 22, & 23 to Malostranské náměstí.

For **Petřín** and **Stromovka** *see p59, p118, & p146;* for the gardens of the **Lobkowicz** and **Wallenstein palaces** *see p92, p111 & pp112–13.* The castle gardens are included in the description of **Hradčany** *(see pp54–5),* and for those of **Letná,** *see pp50–51.*

The Royal Gardens on the slopes of Hradčany

Walk: Letná Park and the Royal Gardens

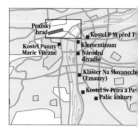

This walk takes you above the left bank of the Vltava, away from the bustle and pollution of the city centre, allowing you to breathe the purer air of Letna and the Královská zahrada (Royal Gardens). (*Follow orange numbers on map for route; for green numbers see* Walk *on pp66–7).*
Allow 2 hours.

Start from Čechův most (nearest tram stop: Právnická Fakulta, No. 17).

1 Čechův Most

The bridge has an attractive early 20th-century design, with angels on columns at each end, sunburst-topped lamp-stands, and Art Nouveau railings.
Cross the busy nábřeží Edvarda Beneše at the far side and climb the steep, zig-

Statue in Hanavský Pavilion

zagging double flight of steps up to Letenské sady (Letná Park).

2 Letenské Sady

The vantage point on the top of the steps once boasted the largest Stalin monument in the Eastern Bloc (30m high). After Krushchev denounced Stalin, it was blown up. Where Stalin once stood, there is now a gigantic 'metronome sculpture' intended to symbolise the return to democracy. In the hillside beneath your feet is a nuclear bunker – the least deserving members of the population planned to retire here in the event of Armageddon. It was actually used to house the city's potato supply. The view over the bridges on the Vltava and Staré Město is stunning.

3 Hanavský Pavilón

A short walk south brings you to the extravagantly ornate Hanavský Pavilón (Pavilion), originally erected for the Paris World Exhibition of 1878, and re-erected here in 1898. It has a charming little café on the terrace, and a good, if expensive restaurant.

Walk on south through leafy Letná until you come to the footbridge over Badeniho, beyond which the Belvedér (Belvedere Palace) can be seen, shrouded in trees at the end of an alley. A detour to the right before reaching the footbridge down Gogolova and across the junction brings you to the Bílkova vila at Mickiewiczova 1, former home and studio of František Bílek. His interesting symbolist sculptures and the furniture he designed himself are on display.

4 Belvedér

The Královský letohrádek (Summer Palace) or Belvedere (see p34) was built on the orders of Ferdinand I as a gift to his wife, Queen Anna. Its terrace was used by Rudolf II's Danish astronomer, Tycho Brahe. In the garden on the west side of this lovely Renaissance building is the bronze 'singing fountain', so-called because of the sound of its gently splashing water.

5 Královská Zahrada

The Royal Gardens (open: May–Sep, Tue–Sun 10am–6pm, admission charge) form one of the best kept parks of Prague. Experimental modern sculptures (said to have been personally chosen by President Havel) mingle with formal parterres, lawns, and noble trees. Halfway up on the left is the Míčovna (Ball Game Court) with sgraffiti decoration on the exterior walls. Parallel to the gardens, to the southeast, is the Jelení přikop (former 'Deer Moat'), where the kings used to corral their red deer. At the southwest end is the Lví dvůr (Lion's Court). This was once Rudolf II's menagerie, where lions and tigers were kept in cages that had to be provided with luxurious and expensive heating against the bitter Prague winters. You come out of the gardens at the west end, opposite the Baroque Jízdárna Pražského hradu (former Riding School) that is now used for exhibitions. Leaving the Prašny most ('Powder Bridge') that leads into the castle complex on your left, turn right along U Prašného mostu for Mariánské hradby and the Nos 22 or 23 trams.

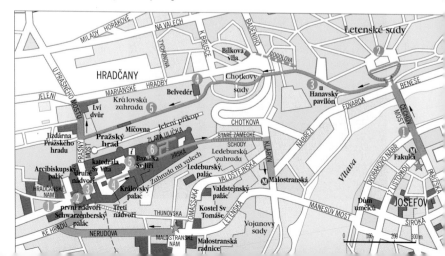

There's little difference between young Czechs and other nationalities. With a trendy club scene (Radost FX has been voted one of the world's best clubs), cinemas, pleasantly seedy clubs in Prague 3, and a rich choice of outdoor activities, the fact that central Prague is tourist-packed and (sometimes) prohibitively expensive is not perhaps the end of the world. Many young Czechs travel abroad, something that the older generation was unable to do. For older Czechs, the good life means taking comfort in good jazz and good beer. Older people also stick to traditional pleasures.

In the city's highly democratic beer cellars, where professors sit cheek-by-jowl with bricklayers and shop assistants, men unwind after a day's work. However, many former dens have metamorphosed into more expensive wine and cocktail bars, chic cafés, and tourist-magnet pubs. To find the beery haunts (badly-lit), you'll need to stray from the centre. Coffee-house culture has suffered since its days of glory in the First Republic, but several old stalwarts, such as Malostranská Kavárna or Café Slavia, still manage to hold their own, while others, such as Café Montmartre, have been gloriously revived.

Despite low salaries, many Praguers own a *chata* (chalet) or *chalupa* (cottage) in the country. On summer weekends, the motorway is jammed as everyone heads out of the city for these, often self-built, second homes. Czechs are also zealous hikers. The areas around Prague and all the national parks are liberally signposted with routes for ramblers. Those who want to join them, will find the *Praha okolí* – environs of Prague – of the *Souboru turistických* map series useful.

All Czechs, whether young or old, enjoy the good life

Hradčany

The term Hradčany is used to describe the whole area of the western hill above Malá Strana. It consists of Pražský hrad (the castle hill complex) and the former town of Hradčany to the west and north of it (*see pp70–71*), with Hradčanské náměstí (Hradčany Square, *see pp68–9*) as its focal point. The Pražský hrad (Prague Castle) towers over the Vltava just where an ancient trade route traversed the river. In the late 9th century, it was fortified by Duke Bořivoj, and has been the spiritual and political focus of the territory of the current Czech lands since.

Standing proud at the main gate, Prague Castle

Pražský Hrad (Prague Castle)

After its diminutive and graceful beginnings in the Romanesque period (Bazilika Sv Jiří, St George's Basilica, and a rotunda Kostel Sv Víta, Church of St Vitus), the architecture of Prague Castle reached its zenith under Charles IV (1346–78), when Matthew of Arras and Petr Parléř (Peter Parler) were at work on the great Gothic cathedral. In the late 14th century, King Vladislav Jagiello commissioned the castle's finest secular architecture from Benedikt Ried – the jousting hall in the Royal Palace. The Habsburgs' architectural legacy, apart from the Belvedere and the Royal Gardens, is depressingly pervasive. The castle area was clad in a barracks-like Baroque classicism by Maria Theresa's architect, Nicolo Pacassi. The last architect of distinction to work on the buildings and gardens was Josip Plečnik, who was commissioned in the 1920s by Czechoslovakia's first president, Tomáš Masaryk, to remodel some of the Baroque features and the bastions.

The castle lies at the heart of Czech consciousness and of Central European culture and history. It has seen imperial grandeur, and played host to humanist scholars, alchemists, and occultists under the eccentric Rudolf II. It has been likened to Kafka's fictional castle under the Communists' rule of darkness; now it is the ceremonial residence of a democratic head of state.

První Nádvoří (First Courtyard)

The tall wrought-iron gates of the entrance are topped by copies of battling Titans by the Baroque sculptor, Ignaz Platzer. There is a changing of the guard every hour, from 5am to 11pm, and a solemn fanfare at noon. The noon fanfare, played from the first floor windows, was composed by rock star Michal Kocáb, who subsequently became an MP.

Zahrada Na Baště (Garden on the Bastion)

The entrance to the left of the main

gateway leads to the Bastion Garden, remodelled by Josip Plečnik in 1927. It has two levels connected by a circular stairway. The Neo-Classical pavilion is by Plečnik's successor as castle architect, Otto Rottmayer.

Druhé Nádvoří (Second Courtyard)

This is entered through the early-Baroque Matyášova brána (Matthias Gate), originally free-standing, later incorporated into Pacassi's rebuilding plan. In the north corner are the Rudofova galerie (Rudolf Gallery) and the Španělský sál (Spanish Hall), whose sumptuous Neo-Baroque interiors are not normally open to the public, although classical concerts are held in the latter. From the northern exit of the castle, access is gained to Obrazárna Pražského hradu (Castle Gallery), containing the remnants of Rudolf II's art collection. This outstanding collection once consisted of 3,000 pictures and 2,500 sculptures, but most of it was looted by the Swedes in 1648. Joseph II sold off much of the rest

(Titian's *Leda and the Swan* was listed in the inventory as *Nude Being Bitten by an Angry Goose*). Among the remains is a bust of Rudolf by Adrian de Vries, and works by Titian, Guido Reni, and Rubens.

Castle Gallery open: Tue–Sun 9am–5pm. Admission charge.

Kaple Svatého Kříže (Chapel of the Holy Cross)

The building in the southeast corner is Anselmo Lurago's Chapel of the Holy Cross, given its Neo-Classical aspect when it was altered in the 19th century. Formerly the Treasury, it has become a somewhat dreary art gallery.

Pražský hrad, 119 08 Praha I, Hradčany. The courtyards and streets of Castle Hill are open until late in the evening.
The castle building is open: daily Nov–Mar, 5am–11pm, Apr–Oct 5am–midnight; gardens open: Apr–Oct 5am–midnight.
The **Information Office** can be found on the third courtyard (*tel: (02) 2437 3368*). Tickets can be bought here and guided tours arranged.

Count the steps to Hradčany, which rises above Malá Strana

Katedrala Svateho Vita (St Vitus' Cathedral)

The earliest church on the site of St Vitus (third courtyard of Prague Castle) was a small Romanesque rotunda, founded by Duke (later Saint) Wenceslas around 925. The choice of St Vitus as the church's dedicatee may have been connected with the fact that the similarly sounding pagan god 'Svantovit' was previously worshipped here. Wenceslas also got a valuable propaganda boost for the new sanctuary in the form of St Vitus' arm, donated by the King of Saxony. Four centuries later, Charles IV, who collected relics as lesser men collect postage stamps, was able to secure the rest of St Vitus for his treasury. This was a major coup, for the cult of this highly prophylactic saint (invoked against epilepsy and 'St Vitus' dance' or chorea) was hugely popular in the Middle Ages.

In 1039, the bones of the most important local martyr, St Adalbert, were also placed in the rotunda. It thus became a much frequented pilgrimage shrine; so much so that a larger church had to be built in 1060 – a towered Romanesque basilica dedicated to Saints Vitus, Adalbert, and Wenceslas, whose tombs were inside. Some remains of the original rotunda and basilica came to light in the 1920s as the cathedral was undergoing its last phase of building. They can be seen below the cathedral floor.

Open: daily Apr–Oct 9am– 5pm, Nov–Mar 9am–4pm. Crypt open: 9am– 4.45pm. Admission charge.

The Building of the Gothic Church

When Prague became an archbishopric in 1344, the future Charles IV summoned Matthew of Arras from Avignon to build a cathedral in the severe Gothic style of contemporary church architecture in France. When he died in 1352, he had completed eight chapels. In 1356 Petr Parléř, a Swabian, took over the work, and it is to his genius that we owe the altogether overwhelming power and beauty of St Vitus' architecture. In particular, it is his vision that produced the striking contrast between the complex ornateness of the exterior walls, and the calm immensity of the interior.

By 1366, Parléř had completed the Chapel of St Wenceslas. The choir was consecrated in 1385, at which time a 'temporary' wall was erected between it and the nave (which was still under construction). Little did the optimistic builders imagine that this wall would still be in place nearly five centuries later!

Parléř and his workshop began the triforium, with its busts of dynastic and other figures, and laid the foundation stone for the great South Tower in 1392. After he died in 1399, his sons Wenceslas and John worked on for 20 years.

The Hussite wars (*see p38*) brought building to a halt, but there was a

Bronze sculptures adorning St Vitus' Cathedral

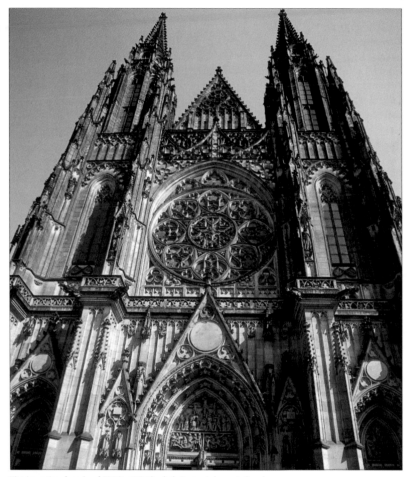

The imposing façade of St Vitus' Cathedral, Prague's largest church

final phase of Gothic construction under King Vladislav Jagiello, whose architect designed the unusual Royal Oratory, built in the 1480s.

In 1843 the Association for the Completion of St Vitus' Cathedral was set up to raise funds. In the second half of the 19th century, Josef Mocker carried through plans that respected the spirit of Parléř's Gothic design, but also managed to salvage important Renaissance and Baroque features that had been added over the years. Work continued into the 20th century, and it was not until the 1929 millennial anniversary celebrations of the murder of St Wenceslas that the entire church was and finally dedicated.

Entrance, Spire, and Stairway

On entering the third courtyard of the castle you are confronted with the cathedral's main entrance in its Neo-Gothic western section, but walk round to the south side to admire Petr Parléř's fine architecture. He built the Gothic part of the 96-m high bell tower, which is topped by a Renaissance gallery and Pacassi's Baroque spire. To the right is the triple-arched Golden Portal, and higher up, a remarkable openwork stairway which is a good example of the unconventional boldness of Parléř's design.

Kaple Sv Václav (St Wenceslas Chapel)

Immediately on your right as you enter through the south portal is the chapel built to hold the remains of Bohemia's most beloved patron saint. Some 1,370 precious stones are set in its lower walls, perhaps signifying the year it was completed. Frescoes depict the New Heavenly Jerusalem, the Life of Wenceslas, and the Passion of Our Lord; there is also a statue of the saint by Parléř's nephew, Heinrich,

and the (much restored) Wenceslas tomb. The Crown Jewels are kept above the chapel but are seldom on view to the public.

The Royal Oratory

Beyond the two chapels to the east of the St Wenceslas chapel is the Royal Oratory, a hanging vault with intricate Gothic decoration which resembles the branches of a tree. Designed for Vladislav Jagiello, it was connected with the king's bedroom in the palace by a covered gangway. The Baroque figure on the left-hand edge represents a miner from the silver mines at Kutná Hora (*see p140*).

The Tomb of St John Nepomuk

Two chapels further on is the Baroque tomb of St John Nepomuk by Fischer von Erlach the Younger (1736). The cherub on the lid is pointing to the saint's tongue, a reference to the Jesuit claim that this part of his remains had never decayed. (According to legend the saint refused to betray the secrets of the Queen's confession to Wenceslas IV.)

ST WENCESLAS

The door of the chapel has a lion's-head knocker to which, it is claimed, the dying Wenceslas clung when struck down by his brother Boleslav. The murder took place 20km outside Prague at Stará Boleslav. The motives for the killing appear to have been dynastic and political rather than religious; nevertheless, Wenceslas was treated as a martyr. His remains were subsequently transferred to St Vitus, apparently by a repentant Boleslav. JM Neale's famous carol (which promotes Duke Wenceslas to king) is unhistorical, although the image of him as a just and merciful ruler may have had some substance.

Panel Reliefs

In the north ambulatory, opposite Parléř's Old Sacristy, is a finely carved oak panel with a relief depicting the Elector Frederick's retreat from Prague after the defeat of the Protestant Bohemians at the White Mountain. A complementary panel in the south ambulatory shows Protestants plundering the cathedral in 1619.

Other Sights of Interest

In the centre of the cathedral is the Royal Mausoleum, a fine Renaissance work with reliefs of Bohemian kings. Next to it is the entrance to the crypt, and archaeological remains of the two earlier churches on this site. The third chapel from the west end on the north wall contains Alfons Mucha's stained-glass window of Saints Cyril and Methodius. Next to it is František Bílek's remarkable *Crucifixion* (1899).

Finally, it is worth taking binoculars to see the 21 sandstone busts by the Parléř school high up in the triforium.

Petr Parléř's soaring triple-arched Golden Portal to St Vitus' Cathedral

Hradčany–Pražský Hrad

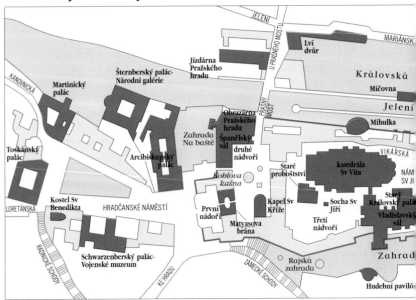

Zahrada Na Valech
(Rampart Garden)

On the south side of the third
courtyard, a flight of steps gives access
to the Rampart Garden with a viewing
terrace by Josip Plečnik (1924). At the
west end it merges with the Rajská
Zahrada (Paradise Garden), changed by
Plečnik, but originally laid out in 1562.

Starý Královský Palác
(Old Royal Palace)

On the southeast side of the third
courtyard is the entrance to the Royal
Palace of the Bohemian rulers between
the 11th and 16th centuries. The top
part was chiefly built by Benedikt Ried
for King Vladislav Jagiello in the 15th
century. Ried was responsible for the
Vladislavský Sál (Vladislav Hall),
entered from the antechamber. On the

way, note the Green Room to your left,
once the Supreme Court, and Vladislav's
Bedchamber. This great space (16m
wide, 62m long, 13m high) was
constructed between 1493 and 1502 in
the late-Gothic style as a jousting and
banqueting hall. In Rudolf II's time, the
space was used as a bazaar and, since
1918, the presidents of the republic have
been sworn in here. Light streams in
from the huge Renaissance windows on
either side.

The door in the southwest corner
gives access to the Bohemian
Chancellery in the Louis Wing of the
palace, scene of the third defenestration
of Prague in 1618. After returning to the
Vladislav Hall, walk to the far end where
there is a viewing platform offering fine
views over Prague. East of the hall is the
rather dreary Kostel Všech svatých (All

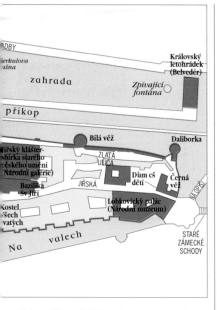

the work of Bonifaz Wohlmut (1563). Portraits of 18th- and 19th-century Habsburgs adorn the walls. To the left is the Riders' Staircase, up which the knights rode to their tournaments in the great hall. At the bottom are the earlier Gothic and Romanesque parts of the palace, where copies of some of the busts on the triforium of St Vitus are displayed, together with models of the historical development of the castle.

Open: Tue–Sun 9am–5pm.
Admission charge.

Saints Chapel). More interesting is the Hall of the Diet in the northeast corner,

> With an entrance ticket, you can visit:
> **St Vitus Cathedral** (including the historic areas)
> **The Old Royal Palace**
> **St George's Basilica**
> **The Powder Tower**
> Open daily from 9am–5pm (4pm in winter). Tickets can be purchased at any of the above sites, or from the Prague Castle Information Centre (third courtyard).

The vaulted ceiling of the Vladislav Hall

Jiřské Náměstí

Leaving the Royal Palace
by the Riders' Staircase
you enter Jiřské náměstí
(St George's Square).

Klášter Sv Jiří (Convent of St George)

In the northeast corner of
the square is the Convent
of St George. Its
foundation in 973 marked
the elevation of Prague to a
bishopric, and its first
abbess was Mlada, sister of
the then ruler, Boleslav II.
It remained a convent for
Benedictine nuns until
Joseph II turned it into
barracks in 1782. Since

Outside St George's
Basilica

BOHEMIA'S FIRST MARTYR

Duke Wenceslas'
grandmother
Ludmila was bitterly
resented by his mother
Drahomira for her
influence over her
grandson. Ludmila was
forced to retire from
Prague to Tetín near
Karlštejn, where she was
murdered by Drahomira's
mercenaries in September
921. Over her grave a
church was built
dedicated to the
Archangel Michael, so
that all miracles that
occurred could be
ascribed to him instead.

In 925 Wenceslas had
the remains of his grand-
mother brought to Prague
and ceremonially
deposited in St George's
Basilica. They proved to
be undecayed, and even
gave off an agreeable
odour, two indisputable
indications of saintliness.

1972 it has housed the National Gallery's Collection of early Czech art and Gothic panel paintings. (*See p108.*) *Jiřske náměstí 33. Tel: (02) 5732 0889. Open: Tue–Sun 10am–6pm. Admission charge. Trams: 22 & 23.*

Bazilika Sv Jiří
(Basilica of St George)

Adjoining the convent to the south is the Basilica of St George. Restoration at the turn of the 20th century and in the 1960s has made this Prague's best preserved Romanesque building, although it has inevitably lost some of its ancient lustre.

Inside there are three aisles, the middle one a great, barn-like hall with a flat wooden ceiling. At the east end a triumphal arch frames a raised altar approached by a double flight of Baroque steps. In front of the steps are the tombs of Boleslav II and Duke Vratislav (the founder of the church), and between them is the entrance to the 12th-century crypt.

The origins of the church go back to the early history of Prague, to about the begining of the 10th century. The last alterations were carried out in 1680, when the chapel of St John Nepomuk was built at the southwest end and the somewhat incongruous Baroque façade was added.

At the southeast end is the chapel dedicated to St Ludmila, Bohemia's first martyr. It contains her tomb, designed by Petr Parléř, and frescoes depicting her life and martyrdom, executed by JV Hellich (1858).
Open: daily 9am–5pm (4pm in winter). Admission charge.

Lobkovický Palác
(Lobkovic Palace)

South of the basilica at Jiřská ulice No. 1 is the former seat of the Lobkowiczes, who were fervent protagonists of the Counter-Reformation. In 1618, the redoubtable Polyxena of Lobkovic took in the two councillors ejected by Protestant nobles from a Chancellery window, and refused entry to their pursuers. Two floors of the palace are given over to a museum of Czech history, including copies of the coronation jewels.
Jiřská ulice 3. Museum of the History of Bohemia open: daily (except Mon), 9am–5pm. Admission charge.

Inside St George's Basilica

The diminutive houses of Golden Lane

Zlatá Ulička (Golden Lane)

At the north end of the castle complex (approached from the rear of St George's Convent) is Golden Lane. The emperor's 24 gatekeepers originally lived in its little houses, pursuing various crafts and trades to eke out their miserable wages. Later, goldsmiths and other artisans arrived. The Renaissance house backing on to the south side of the lane belonged to the *burgrave* (the king's deputy).

No. 22, occupied by Franz Kafka from 1916–17, now belongs to the Kafka society. Nobel Prize-winning poet, Jaroslav Seifert, also lived in Golden Lane.

Prašná Věž/Mihulka (Mihulka or Powder Tower)

At the western end of Golden Lane is the Powder Tower, part of the 13th-century castle fortifications and, later, where Rudolf II's alchemists laboured to find the formula for making gold. Among those who worked on this doomed project were the Englishmen John Dee (formerly employed by Elizabeth I) and Edward Kelley. They were both later disgraced for failing to deliver the goods. Kelley was to end up a prisoner in the castle of Křivoklát (*see p139*). On display are the alchemists' equipment, and a bell foundry.

The appellation 'Mihulka' apparently refers to the lampreys (*mihule*) bred here for the royal kitchens.
Open: Tue–Sun 9am–5pm.
Admission charge.

Daliborka Věž (Dalibor Tower)

This tower, built in 1436 by Benedict Rejt at the east end of the lane, was used as a jail until the end of the 18th century. It takes its name from the nobleman imprisoned there in 1498 on suspicion of aiding and abetting a peasants' revolt near Leitmeritz. Legend says he passed the days before his execution playing the violin so movingly that passers-by filled the basket he let down from his window with victuals and money. Bedřich Smetana used the story for one of his best-known operas, *Dalibor*.
Closed to visitors.

Bílá Věž (the White Tower) and Černá Věž (the Black Tower)

The White Tower (midway along Golden

Lane) and the Black Tower at the eastern tip of the castle were prisons, the latter for debtors. The legend goes that the 16th-century aristocrat Katharine Lažan died in the White Tower, accused of having murdered several young female servants in order to retain her beauty by washing in their maidenly blood.

You can stroll along the passage linking the towers, with arrow-slit views, and lined with lurid shields and heavy suits of armour.

The imposing solid-stone facade of the Charles Bridge Town

Walk: A Stroll through Castle Hill

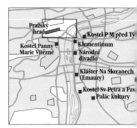

Pražský hrad (Prague Castle) was the spiritual and political focus of the city for most of its history. There has been a fortress and a church here since the 9th century, and from the 12th century until the Republic it was officially the seat of the kings of Bohemia. A detailed description of the buildings is given on pages 54–67 (*see green numbers on map on p51 for the route*). If you want to take just a short stroll, allow about an hour; comprehensive sightseeing requires at least half a day, if not more.

Approach Hradčany up Nerudova and Ke Hradu from Malostranské náměstí (trams 12 & 22).

1 Hradčanské Náměstí

Hradčany Square (*see pp68–9*) is flanked by noble buildings such as the Arcibiskupský palác (Archbishop's Palace) on the north side. Its late incumbent, the heroic Cardinal Tomášek, lived just long enough to see the collapse of the godless regime he withstood. Karl Schwarzenberg, the scion of the former owners of the Schwarzenberský palác (Schwarzenberg Palace) on the south side, enjoyed a remarkable tenure as personal advisor to President Havel. Havel's influence is clearly visible in the uniforms of the guards on duty below the statues of battling giants atop the first gateway. The costume designer for Miloš Forman's *Amadeus* was commissioned by the president to design the Ruritanian outfits.

2 První Nádvoří

The two huge flagstaffs in the První nádvoří (First Courtyard) are made from fir trees, and date from the remodelling of the castle area by the Slovene architect, Josip Plečnik, during the First Republic. Ahead you can see the plain Baroque façade of the Presidential Apartments (to the south), and (to the north) the Spanish Hall and Castle Gallery. All this, together with the east wing of the next courtyard, is the work of Maria Theresa's architect, Nicolo Pacassi.
Pass through the Matthias Gate.

3 Druhé Nádvoří

The Matyášova brána (Matthias Gate), leading to the Druhé nádvoří (Second Courtyard), is a triumphal arch named after the brother of Rudolf II. The Neo-Classical building on the right is the Kaple Svatého Kříže (Chapel of the Holy Cross), once the treasury, now a gallery.

4 Třetí Nádvoří

The Třetí nádvoří (Third Courtyard), beyond, is dominated by the Katedrála Svatého Víta (Cathedral of St Vitus). Walk across the space to get a better view of the South Tower, and the early Gothic architecture of the eastern end of this great edifice constructed by Petr Parléř and his sons. If you walk on through the courtyard, the Královský palác (Old Royal Palace), with its celebrated Vladislavský sál (Vladislav Hall) and Riders' Staircase, is ahead of you. On the right, Plečnik's green cylindrical canopy entices you down some steps to the Rampart Gardens. *Enter Jiřské náměstí.*

5 Bazilika Svatého Jiří

The last courtyard – St George's Square – contains the Basilica of St George, one of the finest surviving Romanesque buildings in Central Europe. The origins of this and the adjacent monastery lie in the 10th century. The basilica regularly hosts chamber music concerts. The monastery houses the National Gallery's collection of early Bohemian art.
Now take Jiřská, beside the church, and turn left as soon as you can to reach the famous Zlatá ulička (Golden Lane).

6 Zlatá Ulica

In the 19th century, the tiny 16th-century houses that line the street were supposed to have been the dwellings of Rudolf II's alchemists. Franz Kafka also lived here for a while. Prepare to find the lane densely packed with tourists.
Return to Jiřská and descend the steps at the northwestern tip of Castle Hill, which lead eventually to Klárov, the Malostranská metro station, and to the No. 22 tram.

Statue of St George, Prague Castle

Hradčanské Náměstí

Hradčany Square

The township of Hradčany dates back to 1320 and originally consisted of little more than the square itself (*see p54 & p68*). Following a devastating fire in 1541, most of the burghers' houses were pulled down by the Catholic nobility, who bought up large plots and built great palaces on them. In the centre of the square is Ferdinand Brokoff's Marian Column (1726), with representations of the Bohemian patron saints around its base. To the west of the Arcibiskupský palác (Archbishop's Palace), look out for a cast-iron candelabra gaslight dating from the 1860s.

The Archbishop's Palace, with its magnificent façade, is a masterpiece of Rococo design

Schwarzenberský Palác (Schwarzenberg Palace)

At No. 2 on the south side of the square, the Schwarzenberg Palace has a number of striking Italianate features, including Lombardy cornices and Renaissance sgraffiti. When Agostino Galli originally built it for the Lobkowiczes in 1563, seven existing houses on the site had to be demolished. Inside (on the second floor) are exquisitely detailed tempera frescoes depicting scenes from Homer.

The Schwarzenbergs acquired the building only in 1719. A previous owner became famous for having invited Tycho Brahe (the imperial mathematician) to a party in 1601. It proved to be his last outing: according to the story, as a result of over-indulgence at dinner, his bladder burst on the way home.

The Vojenské Historické Muzeum (Military History Museum) is located here. (It is currently under re-construction and closed to the public.)

Arcibiskupský Palác (Archbishop's Palace)

Close to the castle's gates is the Archbishop's Palace at No. 16, boasting an elegant Rococo façade by Johan Wirch (1764). Traces of Jean-Baptiste Mathey's earlier Baroque design (1676) may be seen in the entrance portals and the tympanum rising above the middle of the façade. With this first commission in Prague, Mathey introduced many of the architectural principles of the Italian Baroque he imbibed from Rome.

The original Renaissance palace on this site was presented by Ferdinand I to the first post-Hussite archbishop of Prague, whose residence thus moved closer to the centre of power at Pražský hrad. Bonifaz Wohlmut had it rebuilt in 1564.

The palace is open to the public only once a year on Maundy Thursday from 9am–5pm.

Šternberský Palác (Sternberg Palace)

The left-hand entrance arch of the Archbishop's Palace leads to the Sternberg Palace, at No. 15, a building of the high Baroque designed by Giovanni Alliprandi. The Chinoiserie room on the second floor is notable, but the main reason for visiting the palace is the National Gallery's collection of old European art (*see p108*).
Open: Tue–Sun 10am–6pm.
Tel: (02) 2051 4598. Free admission every first Wed in the month.

Martinický Palác (Martinic Palace)

Restoration during 1971 brought to light sgraffiti depicting the story of Joseph and Potiphar on the impressive Renaissance façade of the Martinic Palace (No. 8). Its owner from 1624 was Jaroslav Bořita of Martinitz, one of the councillors defenestrated from the Bohemian Chancellery in 1618. He was later made a count for his troubles. Both he and his fellow victim, Vilém Slavata, arranged to have their miraculous escape immortalised in bombastic sculptures for their palaces.
The palace is not open to the public.

Toskanský Palác (Tuscany Palace)

This huge and rather sombre palace, at the west end of the square (No. 5), was built by Jean-Baptiste Mathey in 1689–91, and owned by the Dukes of Tuscany between 1718 and 1918. It now belongs to the Czech Foreign Ministry.

Renaissance sgraffiti on the Schwarzenberg Palace

Walk: Hradčany Hinterland

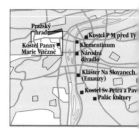

The tranquil backwater of the Castle District seems frozen in time. The bustling medieval town fell victim to the great fire of 1541, but in the 17th century the Catholic beneficiaries of the Counter-Reformation built grandiose palaces which still abound.

Allow 2½ hours.

The walk begins in Hradčanské náměstí, reached via Nerudova and Ke Hradu from Malostranské náměstí (trams 12 & 22). If you are not up to a steep climb, take the funicular to the top and enjoy the walk down.

1 Hradčanské Náměstí

Apart from the Arcibiskupský palác (Archbishop's Palace) and the Schwarzenberský palác (Schwarzenberg Palace – *see p68),* the western end of the square is dominated by the Toskánský palác (Tuscany Palace). North of it, on the corner of Kanovnická, is the more modest Martinický palác (Martinic Palace), notable for its lively sgraffito decoration. In the centre of the square is a Baroque Marian Column, erected in thanksgiving for deliverance from the plague. Also worth a look is the heavily ornate wrought-iron street lamp, one of two in Prague.

Walk west along Loretánská, and turn right down to the shrine of Loreta.

2 The Loreta

The Loreta is inspired by the famous Italian original (Loreto) that claims to possess the Santa Casa, the house in Nazareth where the Annunciation took place. The most entertaining part is the cloisters, lined with saints whose responsibilities range from curing gallstones (St Liborius) to the return of lost property (St Anthony). The Loreta contains pictures of scenes from the life of the Virgin, and claims to possess beams and a brick from the real Loreto. The Church of the Nativity is notable for the depiction of St Agatha carrying her severed breasts on a plate, and the treasury for an outrageously over-the-top diamond monstrance designed by Fischer von Erlach. (*See also pp72–3.*)

Walk back up to the junction with Pohořelec and turn right.

3 Černínský Palác

On the corner is the vast, rusticated façade of the Cernín Palace, the largest in Prague. During the First Republic, it was taken over by the Foreign Ministry and it was from here that Jan Masaryk, the only non-Communist left in the cabinet of Klement Gottwald, plunged to his death in suspicious circumstances on 10 March 1948.

Continue down Pohořelec, passing the junction with Úvoz, then turn left into a cobbled square with limes and acacias, around which are grouped the buildings of the Strahovský klášter, see p130.

4 Strahovský Klášter

This is the home of Premonstratensian monks and was founded in 1140. The high point of any visit is the frescoed library, particularly the Philosophical Hall with its painted ceiling (*The History of Humanity*) by Franz Anton Maulpertsch.

Leave the monastery by an archway in the eastern wall and walk south through the Strahov Gardens. The Vltava and Malá Strana unfold before you. In two minutes you see steps to your right, which lead up to Petřín (see below and p118).

5 Petřín

This is an especially pleasant part of the walk, through pear and plum orchards. At the top of the crumbling steps is Prague's mini-Eiffel Tower. Nearby are the Bludiště (Mirror Maze) and the Observatory. From the summit of the hill you can see a section of the so-called Hladová zeď' (Hunger Wall) to the south.

Some say it is said to have been built as a job-creation scheme by Charles IV between 1360 and 1362; others point out that it was paid for by the expropriation of the Jews.

The funicular railway (*lanová dráha*) terminus on the summit is approached through a rose garden. The railway is now electric, but until the 1960s it was worked by water pressure. Halfway down you can alight at Nebozízek Station, where there is the Nebozízek restaurant with another good view.

Descend to Újezd, where you can pick up trams to the city centre.

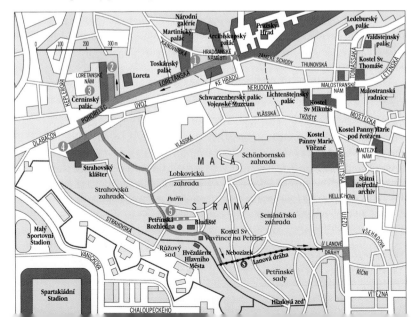

The Loreta

After the Catholic victory at the battle of the White Mountain (1620), the Czech lands were swept by a wave of pietism. To eradicate nostalgia for Protestant heresies and heroes, the formidable propaganda machine of the Counter-Reformation was turned up full blast. In particular, the Marian cult was exploited, replacing Protestant hostility to images with a mixture of symbolism, sensuality, and superstition.

Mariolatry was given its first major impetus in Bohemia with the founding of the Prague Loreto by the Spanish-born Benigna Kateřina Lobkowicz in 1626. The focus of the sanctuary was an imitation of the Santa Casa, claimed to be the historical house of the Virgin Mary, originally in Nazareth, but deposited by angels on Italian shores in a laurel grove (Loreto) near Ancona. This legend appealed to public imagination: countless 'Loretos' sprang up in Catholic Europe, and eventually there were some 50 in Bohemia alone.

The West Façade

Designed by Christoph Dientzenhofer, the outer wing was completed by his son Kilián in 1726. The rich decoration on the façade is crowned by a kneeling Virgin Mary (above the left-hand gable), and by the Angel of the Annunciation (over the right-hand gable). Below are the four evangelists and St Christopher. The coat of arms of the shrine's patrons, Prince Philipp Lobkowicz and his wife, are above the entrance.

The Clocktower

A carillon in the clocktower plays the

Baroque tower above the Loreta shrine

Marian hymn 'We Greet Thee a Thousand Times' every hour on the hour. The mechanism was made in Amsterdam and consists of 27 bells collectively weighing about 1,600kg.

The astronomer Tycho Brahe successfully petitioned Rudolf II to order the monks to ring their evensong carillon before it got dark, as otherwise it disturbed his concentration when stargazing!

The Cloisters

The lower arcade has an upper storey added by Kilián Dientzenhofer in the 1740s. The painted ceilings of the vaults feature motifs from the litany used during processions at Loreto itself. The arcades themselves are lined with beautiful representations of saints with miraculous healing powers, whose fields of expertise are inscribed below their statues. Thus, a sore throat falls under the ambit of St Blaise, toothache will be treated by St Apollonia, and plague by St Roch.

Kostel Narození Páně
(Church of the Nativity)

On the east side of the sanctuary this 18th-century church has a fine fresco of *Christ in the Temple* by Václav Reiner. Other frescoes by JV Schöpf depict the Christmas scene of the *Three Kings and the Shepherds*.

The Santa Casa

In the middle of the cloisters is the Santa Casa, the spiritual focus of the Loreto, built by Giovanni Orsi and Andrea Allio in 1631. Rich stucco depicts figures from the Old Testament and scenes from the life of the Virgin. A limewood statue of Our Lady encased in elaborate silver decoration glimmers in the dim religious light.

The Treasury

On the first floor is the fabulous treasury, whose loveliest work is a diamond monstrance (1699), designed by Johann Fischer von Erlach and made by Viennese silversmiths. The dramatic and sensual representation of the joint victory of Maria Immaculata and the Trinity over the forces of evil is a stunning example of Baroque extravagance. It is said that many of its 6,222 diamonds came from the court dress of the benefactress, Countess Kolowrat, who left her entire fortune to Loreto.

Loretánské náměstí (Hradčany).
Tel: (02) 2451 0780. Open: Tue–Sun 9am–noon, 1–4.30pm. Admission charge. Tram: 22 to Památník pisemnictvi.

Old Town Prague is a magnificent symphony of spires and towers

Josefov

The Jews started arriving in Prague in the 10th century and settled on both sides of the Vltava. Their first eviction was at the hands of Otakar II, who needed their land for his new town of Malá Strana on the west bank. From that time until the deportations to concentration camps under the Nazis, theirs was a history of recurrent victimisation and violence. Now only about 2,000 Jews are said to live in Prague.

Exhibitions are held in the Ceremonial Hall

The two worst pogroms of the Middle Ages were in 1086, when the Crusaders indulged in an orgy of Jew-killing, and 1389, when 3,000 Jews were massacred over Easter. In 1745, Maria Theresa expelled the Jewish population from Prague, but had to allow them back soon afterwards under pressure from commercial interests. Joseph II's 'Edict of Tolerance' in 1781 somewhat

Interior of Maisel Synagogue

improved their lot, but with the rise of Czech nationalism in the 19th century, many German-speaking Jews found themselves on the wrong side of the cultural divide. Nevertheless, in the first half of the 20th century, German Jewish literary culture flourished, producing a string of major writers including Franz Kafka, Max Brod, Egon Erwin Kisch, and Franz Werfel.

All that ended with the Nazis, who killed 80,000 of the 90,000 Jews who remained in Bohemia after the invasion. A grotesque footnote to the genocide was Hitler's decision to found, in Prague, a Jewish Museum which he designated an 'Exotic Museum of an Extinct Race'.

Josefov is reached by metro to Staroměstská or tram 17. See Walk on p76.

The Ghetto

The ghetto was built in the 13th century in accordance with the church's view that Jewish dwellings should be kept separate from those of Christians. From time to time, ordinances regarding clothing – designed to mark out Jews – were promulgated. Under Vratislav II they had to wear yellow cloaks; later it was bizarre hats or yellow circles.

Under Rudolf II, whose financial adviser was the Jew Mordechai Maisel, the Jewish community achieved a greater degree of autonomy. The emperor's obsession with the occult also engendered an interest in cabbalistic lore and learning (this was the age of Rabbi Jehuda Löw, credited with creating the 'Golem' – *see p76*).

In 1784, Jewish residence restrictions were abolished following Joseph II's Edict, but by the end of the 19th century the ghetto area had become an insanitary slum and red-light district. In 1893, many buildings were razed to make way for a modern quarter.

STÁTNÍ ŽIDOVSÉ MUZEUM (STATE JEWISH MUSEUM)

A single ticket covers access to all the sights of the State Jewish Museum listed below, with the exception of the seventh, the Old-New Synagogue, which does not form part of the museums.
Office and Jewish museum:
Jáchymovo 3.
Tel: (02) 2481 0099;
www. jewishmuseum.cz
Free admission.
All other sights open:
Sun–Fri 9.30am–
7.30pm. Admission
charge. Tickets available from
the Klausová Synagóga on U
starého hřbitova. Last tickets are

issued half an hour before closing time.
Most monuments close over lunch,
noon–1pm.

Klausová Synagóga (Klausen Synagogue)

This 17th-century building houses a permanent exhibition of Jewish customs and traditions. Rabbi Löw is said to have had his school here.
U starého hřbitova 4.

Maiselová Synagóga (Maisel Synagogue)

Mordechai Maisel gave 12,000 denars for the construction of the synagogue in 1590. This was destroyed by fire and replaced with a new Gothic synagogue, which now houses an exhibition of the History of the Jews in Bohemia and Moravia from the 10th to the18th century.
Maiselova 10.

Obřadní Síň (The Ceremonial Hall)

This Neo-Romanesque building at the Old Jewish Cemetery entrance exhibits Jewish customs and traditions. Some 15,000 Jewish children were held here by the Nazis before being deported to Auschwitz, where the majority perished.
U starého hřbitova.

Universal symbol of Judaism

Pinkasova Synagóga (Pinkas Synagogue)

A Rabbi Pinkas founded the earliest synagogue on this site in 1479; the Gothic vault of the interior was built in 1535, and the women's gallery was added a century later. On its walls are inscribed the names of 77,297 Bohemian and Moravian victims of the holocaust, as well as drawings of children from the Terezin holocaust. *Široká 5.*

Španělská Synagóga (Spanish Synagogue)

The Spanish Synagogue is an Alhambra-like building with Neo-Renaissance features, the work of Ignaz Ullmann (1864). It contains a history of the Jews of Bohemia and Moravia, after their emancipation to the present day. *Vezeusko 1.*

Staronová Synagóga (Old-New Synagogue)

Built between 1270 and 1280 and still in use, this is the most impressive of Josefov's synagogues. The design incorporates an unusual five-ribbed vaulting inside. In the vestibule are chests placed for the collection of taxes.

Over the entrance to the hall is a relief of a vine with 12 bunches of grapes, supposedly representing the 12 tribes of Israel. Inside are the *almemor* (a pulpit behind a Gothic lattice) and a shrine for the Torah (a parchment scroll of the Pentateuch). A magnificent statue of Moses by František Bílek stands next to the synagogue in a small park. *Červená ulice. Open: daily except Sat & Jewish holidays, Apr–Oct 9am–6pm, Fri until 5pm; Nov–Mar 9am–5pm, Fri until 2pm. Free admission.*

Starý Židovský Hřbitov (Old Jewish Cemetery)

Over 550 years the remains of some 100,000 people have been bundled into 12 layers of graves in the Old Jewish Cemetery (*see pp78–9*). The earliest grave is that of poet Avigdor Kara, who survived and chronicled the 1389 pogrom. Also interred here is Mordechai Maisel, who amassed 17,000 gulden from trade monopolies under Rudolf II, and was the ghetto's greatest benefactor. Rabbi Löw's tomb is sprinkled with pebbles, prayers, even money – evidently the old

THE GOLEM LEGEND

In 1580, when the perennial accusations of ritual murders and other crimes were being levelled at the Jews, Rabbi Löw decided that the ghetto needed reassurance and protection. Using his cabbalistic knowledge (so the story goes) he was able to create a humanoid from the mud of the Vltava, the 'Golem' (Hebrew for 'unformed matter'). Its job was to act as servant and bodyguard to the community: when not required, it was switched off by placing a secret formula (*shem*) in its mouth. Like many a later Frankenstein monster, the Golem finally escaped the control of its creator and ran amok in the rabbi's house (Löw had forgotten to put the *shem* in his mouth). For this rebellion, the humanoid was promptly turned back into a lump of clay and deposited in the attic of the Old-New Synagogue.

cabbalist still exerts a spell. The headstones are works of art, with carved symbols indicating the deceased's profession, or the family name.

It is a strange and haunting place, evoking both the forlorn dignity and astonishing resilience of the Jewish community.
Široka.

Vysoká Synagóga
(High Synagogue)

The fine Renaissance interior includes an upstairs, or 'high' prayer hall.
Červená 1. Closed to the public.

Židovská Radnice
(Jewish Town Hall)

The Rococo aspect of the Jewish Town Hall is the result of alterations by Josef Schlesinger in 1765, when it also acquired its backwards-reading Hebraic clock. The hall is still the community centre for Prague's 1,000 Jews, and also boasts a kosher restaurant.

The Nazis employed Jewish scholars here to collect material for the planned 'Exotic Museum of an Extinct Race' (*see p74*) until early 1945, when the last of them were despatched to the camps.
Maiselova 18.

The highly ornamental interior of the Spanish Synagogue

Walk: Josefov

This walk covers the former Jewish ghetto. In 1850 it acquired the name Josefov (Josef's Town, *see pp74–7*) in honour of the Emperor Josef II whose Edict of Tolerance in 1781 lifted many restrictions on Jews. (*Follow green numbers on map on p129 for route.*)
Allow about 1 hour.

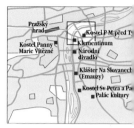

Take tram 17 to the Právnická Fakulta stop near Čechův most. Walk down Pařížská and bear right into Maiselova, then right again into U stárého hřbitova.

Head coverings are offered at the Old-New Synagogue

1 U Starého Hřbitova

Tickets can be purchased for all the sights of Josefov in the Klausová Synagóga (Klausen Synagogue) to your left at the end of the street. The synagogue has a print display with items dating back to 1512, the year when the first Jewish books to be printed anywhere were produced on this site. On the right is the Obřadní síň (Ceremonial Hall) which features pictures by children in the Terezín concentration camp.
Enter Starý židovský hřbitov (Old Jewish Cemetery) by the adjacent gate.

2 Starý Židovský Hřbitov

In Hebrew, the name for this tranquil yet haunting place translates as 'The House of Life'; for over three centuries it was the only permitted burial place of the Prague Jews, so that some 12 layers of mortal remains had to be piled on top of one another *(see p76)*. The most visited tomb is that of the famous scholar Rabbi Löw. Leaving the cemetery on the south side you pass the Pinkasova Synagóga (Pinkas Synagogue). Inside is a memorial to the Czech and Slovak victims of the Holocaust. There are 77,297 names inscribed on a memorial wall, all culled from the Nazis' pedantically precise transport files.

Turn left along Široká and second right back into Maiselova.

3 Maiselova Synagóga

On your left you soon come to the Maisel Synagogue, named after the ghetto's most famous mayor, who was also Rudolf II's minister of finance. Inside is a display of ritualistic objects, such as circumcision instruments, and combs used in preparing the dead for burial.

Retrace your steps along Maiselova as far as the junction, on your right, with Červená.

4 Červená

On your right is the diminutive Rococo Židovská radnice (Jewish Town Hall). The cream and pink building's most notable feature is a Jewish clock on the front with a Hebrew dial, the hands of which move anti-clockwise (Hebrew script also goes from right to left). The Town Hall is the centre of the Jewish community and incorporates a kosher restaurant.

Directly opposite is the Staronová Synagóga (Old-New Synagogue), one of the earliest in Europe, with stepped brick gables and a fine-vaulted Gothic ceiling inside. A wrought-iron surround in the centre encloses the *bimah*, the lectern for readings from the Torah. For men and boys, paper skullcaps must be purchased in the vestibule before entering the sacred area.

Adjoining the Town Hall is the Vysoká Synagóga (High Synagogue), the main exhibition hall of the Jewish Museum.

The Rococo elegance of the Jewish Town Hall

The abundance of Jewish mementoes and official buildings in Josefov is thanks to Hitler's decision to turn this area into an official Nazi display, described as 'An Exotic Museum of an Extinct Race'.

At the end of Červená, turn right into Pařížská, and left into Široká, going as far as Vězeňská.

5 Španělská Synagóga

The Spanish Synagogue on Vězeňská lives up to its name, with its Moorish appearance and Alhambra-like interior. The original synagogue here was founded by Sephardic Jews fleeing the Inquisition.

Return to Pařížská and Čechův most via Dušní and Bílkova.

Ignored in the author's lifetime, burned by the Nazis, and suppressed by the Communists, the works of Franz Kafka (1883–1924) are at last being celebrated in the city of his birth.

Prague, the city that Franz Werfel claimed 'has no reality', looms over Kafka's stories as it did over his life. Praský hrad inspired *The Castle,* and the Hladová zed (Hunger Wall – *see p71 & p119*) on Petřín Hill, his story *The Great Wall of* *China.* Echoes of the Prague ghetto reverberate through the fantastical world of his imagination. The bumbling bureaucracy of the Habsburg administration in the 19th century supplied Kafka with numerous ideas. In retrospect, his vision seems to be a premonition of what life for the people of Prague would be like under Nazism and Stalinism, but Kafka did not live long enough to experience it.

Devotees of Kafka's work can follow his trail through Prague – to his one-time workplace (Na poříčí

7), to the house he rented in Golden Lane on Castle Hill (No. 22), and to his grave in the Jewish Cemetery at Strašnice (Metro line A to Želivského). The city's beauty is all around us, but reading Kafka makes us aware of another, more menacing presence behind the beautiful façade. Kafka had this in mind, perhaps, when he wrote in his diaries: 'Prague is a dear mother with sharp claws: she never lets go of you.'

Facing page above left: memorial to Franz Kafka; right: Hunger Wall; below: Kafka's grave in the Jewish Cemetery; this page above: 22 Golden Lane; below: Number 7 Na Poříčí

The Empire-style U Hybernů is a venue for exhibitions and cultural events

U Hybernů (Hibernian House)

The name of this building recalls the Irish Franciscans who occupied a Baroque monastery and church at this site from 1629 until the dissolution of their establishment under Joseph II in 1786. After briefly being used as a theatre, the former church was reconstructed in Neo-Classical (or 'Empire') style in 1811 to plans by Johann Fischer. The Imperial Government used it as the Central Customs Office for Prague (hence the imperial double-headed eagle in the side-wall tympanum). After World War II it became an exhibition hall. Fischer's design, modelled on the Old Mint in Berlin, is the most completely realised example of Empire style in Bohemia. *Náměstí Republiky 3. Open during exhibitions. Metro: Náměstí Republiky.*

Karolinum
(Carolinum/Charles University)

Charles IV founded Europe's 35th university in Prague on 7 April 1348. The Charles University, or Karolinum, was the first such foundation in Central Europe, and its professors and students were entitled to teach and study at any other school sanctioned by the Catholic church.

This all came into question from 1409 onwards, after the Hussite faction in Prague pressured Wenceslas IV into issuing the Decree of Kutná Hora, whereby the Czechs gained the upper hand in the university administration. There was a mass exodus of non-Bohemians (leading to the founding of Leipzig University), and Jan Hus became rector of a school increasingly regarded elsewhere in Europe as a nest of heretics. Eventually, in 1412, the Catholic interest rallied its forces and succeeded in having Hus ejected.

After the Battle of the White Mountain in 1620, the Jesuits (who had had their own 'Clementinum' since the mid-16th century) were allowed to annex the Carolinum.

The Buildings

Some remains of the original buildings have either been laid bare during modern restoration work or were 're-Gothicised' by Joseph Mocker in the late 19th century. The finest surviving feature is the oriel window (c.1370) overlooking Ovocný trh (the fruit market). Much of the rest was reworked in Baroque style in the 18th century.

The 17th-century Assembly Hall on the first floor, with a tapestry depicting Charles IV and paintings on the organ loft by V Sychra, is unfortunately not always accessible. However, you can visit the much restored Gothic vaults at ground-floor level, now used for exhibitions of contemporary Czech art. In the Grand Courtyard there is a modern statue of Hus by Karel Lidický.

The Carolinum is now the University Rectorate, which has faculties dispersed elsewhere around Prague. Graduation ceremonies take place at Ovocný trh 5. *Železná 9, Staré Město pedestrian zone. Cloister and halls open during exhibitions; otherwise visiting hours are 10am–6pm. Metro: to Můstek or Náměstí Republiky.*

Letohrádek Hvězda (Star Castle)

The Imperial Governor of Bohemia, Ferdinand of Tyrol, himself designed this remarkable Renaissance country house. It was built in the form of a six-pointed star between 1555 and 1557 by Italian architects, and has preserved its original aspect with the exception of the roof, which is 18th-century. Especially attractive features inside are the stucco reliefs of scenes from classical mythology and Roman history. The gods personifying the planets named after them form the focal points on the ceilings of individual rooms. In the cellars are tableaux with explanatory texts about the defenestration of Prague and the Battle of the White Mountain.

After World War II, the castle was sensitively restored by Pavel Janák and now houses fairly numbing displays on the life and work of the historical novelist Alois Jirásek, and the painter Mikoláš Aleš.

Open: Tue–Sat 10am–4pm, Sun 10am–5pm. Admission charge. Trams: 8 & 22 to Vypich (beyond Břevnov).

The aptly named Star Castle, now home to an artist's museum

Karlův Most
Charles Bridge

In high summer, visitors jam the Charles Bridge; neo-hippies and their dogs relax; pretty girls sell knick-knacks; and often a Dixieland jazz band supplies free entertainment. In winter, the freezing mist that rises from the Vltava envelopes the bridge. No other place in the city is more atmospheric, or has richer historical associations.

St John Nepomuk, Prague's most revered saint

Of all Charles IV's ambitious undertakings, which included the building of St Vitus, and the founding of the university and Nové Město, this 516-m long sandstone bridge with its 16 graceful arches captures the imagination most. He laid the foundation stone on 9 July 1357, but did not live to see the great work completed in 1383. That pleasure was reserved for his son Wenceslas IV (who murdered his Vicar-General, John of Nepomuk, by having him thrown off the bridge).

Over the years the Charles Bridge has witnessed many dramatic events. During the Middle Ages, dishonest traders were suspended from the bridge in wicker baskets. In 1621 the heads of the executed Bohemian nobles who had fought against the Habsburgs were exhibited on the tower at the Staré Město end. The bridge served as the venue for the signing of the treaty that put an end to the Thirty Years War.

Architecture and Statuary

The Prague Bridge (it only became the 'Charles Bridge' in 1870) replaced an earlier Romanesque one made of stone, named after Judith of Thuringia, wife of Vladislav I. It is not quite straight, having been built using the Judith Bridge's land foundations on each side of the river, but with midstream piers placed slightly to the south of the previous construction.

The Bridge Towers

All that is left from the Romanesque period are some piers sunk in the riverbed, and the smaller of the two bridge towers at the Malá Strana end, the latter having been rebuilt during the Renaissance era.

It is joined to a higher tower built by King George of Poděbrady, which is largely an imitation of the tower on the opposite bank. At the Staré Město end is the impressive Gothic tower designed by Petr Parléř. St Vitus is portrayed on the east façade, flanked by Charles IV (on the left) and Wenceslas IV (on the right). Above them are St Adalbert and St Sigismund, patron saints of Bohemia, and below them the coats of arms of the Czech Crown Lands, together with a veiled kingfisher, the heraldic symbol of Wenceslas IV.

The Statues

A remarkable feature of the Charles Bridge is the Baroque sculptures of saints, erected between 1683 and 1714 on each side. Originally, there had been only one stark crucifixion scene on the bridge, but in the late 17th century, Bernini's sumptuous statuary for the Ponte dei Angeli in Rome inspired a similar plan for Prague.

The Jesuits, keen to promote the cult of St John Nepomuk, put up his statue by Jan Brokoff (in the middle of the north side) in 1683. The Brokoff dynasty (Jan, Jan Michael, and Ferdinand Maximilian) supplied a number of fine works.

Some of the older statues have been replaced with copies; several uninspired Neo-Gothic works went up in the 19th century. The finest Baroque sculpture is Matthias Braun's representation of St Luitgarde and the Crucifixion (1710) on the south side, the fourth from the Malá Strana bank. A modern work of some distinction is Karel Dvořák's SS *Cyril and Methodius* (1938) on the north side, the fifth from the Staré Město bank. *Trams: 12, 17, 18, 22, or 23. Metro: to Staroměstská or Malostranská.*

A new day dawns on the Charles Bridge

Klementinum (Clementinum)

In 1556, Ferdinand I summoned 40
Jesuit monks to Prague. They took over
the Dominicans' church of St Clement
and founded the Clementinum, a centre
of learning and propaganda for the
faith. It continued to expand up to the
mid-18th century, swallowing up 32
houses, three churches, several gardens,
and even the heretical Carolinum
(*see p82*). After the disbanding of the
Jesuits, the now non-heretical Charles
University moved its library to the
Clementinum. It currently houses the
National Library of the Czech Republic,
and the State Technical Library, with
an estimated 5 million volumes,
numerous incunabula, and manuscripts.
Its most celebrated item is the *Codex
Vyšegradensis* of 1085.

The architects chiefly involved in
building the Clementinum were Carlo
Lurago, Francesco Caratti, and (later)
František Kaňka.

Kostel Sv Kliment
(St Clement's Church)

This is the Prague base of the Uniate
Church (halfway between Orthodoxy
and Catholicism). Entry is difficult, but
it is worth trying in order to see the
frescoes by Jan Hiebel depicting the life
of St Clement, and the fine sandstone
sculptures of the church fathers and the
four evangelists by Matthias Braun.
Open: Fri 5pm, or apply at the sacristy.

The Marian Chapel

František Kaňka completed this chapel
in 1730. The name 'Hall of Mirrors' is a
reference to the mirrors in the ceiling. It
served as the private chapel of the

Plaque to Joseph II on the wall of the
Clementinum

Brotherhood of Our Lady; hence
Hiebel's ceiling fresco depicting the life
of the Virgin. Concerts and exhibitions
are regularly held here.

Vlašská Kaple (The Italian Chapel)

Built in 1597 for the community of
Italian painters, sculptors, and masons
in Prague, the chapel has an elliptical
form inspired by the Roman Baroque. It
still belongs to the Italian state.
*Located between St Clement's and the east
end of the Church of the Holy Saviour on
Karlova. Entry is difficult.*

The Halls

Kaňka and Hiebel designed and
decorated the **Jesuit Library** or 'Baroque
Hall' in the east wing, with its
Salomonic columns and ceiling fresco of
The Temple of Wisdom. Also frescoed by
Hiebel, the **Mathematical Hall** contains
a collection of table clocks.

The **Mozart Room** is a full-blown
example of Rococo, with beautiful
paintings and finely carved bookcases.

Access to the Klementinum is from Karlova or Křížovnická ulice. The Klementinum is being renovated, but some buildings are open, including the Mirror Room.
Tel: (02) 2166 3111.
Trams: 17 & 18 to Staroměstská.

Křižovnické Náměstí
(Knights of the Cross Square)

The Coronation Route of the Bohemian kings passed along Karlova and across the Knights of the Cross Square on to the Charles Bridge, before winding its way through the Lesser Quarter up to the Hrad. The square is named after the hospice Order of the Knights of the Cross with a Red Star, keepers of the Judith Bridge in the 13th century.

Next to the bridgehead is Ernst Hähnel's cast-iron statue of Charles IV. The outbreak of the 1848 revolution in Prague prevented its planned inauguration on the 500th anniversary of the founding of Charles University.

Kostel Sv Františka Serafinského
(The Church of St Francis Seraphicus)

This was the knights' own church (*see p39*). On the street corner is Jan Bendl's statue of St Wenceslas.

Kostel Svatého Salvátora
(The Church of the Holy Saviour)

This Jesuit church on the east side of the square forms part of the Clementinum. It took over a century (1593–1714) to complete. The rich (now blackened and crumbling) statuary on the façade is by Jan Bendl. Carlo Lurago was the main architect, while the lavish stucco inside is the work of Domenico Galli. Karel Stádník's modern (1985) glass and metal altar symbolising the cosmos is in harmony with the interior.
Trams: 17 & 18 to Staroměstská.

The Church of the Holy Saviour's façade is decorated with statues of angels and saints

Walk: Národní Třída to Křížovnické Náměstí

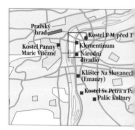

This route encompasses places associated with a vanishing Habsburg empire, an aspiring playwright, aggressive agitators, and astute propagandists.
Allow 1½ hours.

Begin at Národní divadlo (National Theatre), reached by trams 6, 9, 18, & 22.

1 Národní Divadlo

The National Theatre (*see pp100–101*) opened in 1881 with a performance of Smetana's patriotic opera *Libuše*. Opposite it, on the corner of Národní and the embankment, is the Café Slavia.

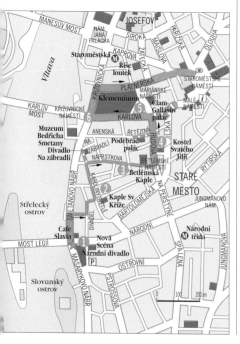

In the inter-war years this was the haunt of literati, including Nobel Laureate Jaroslav Seifert; under the Husák regime, opposition writers met here to pass around their *samizdat* manuscripts.

A few steps to the north on the embankment brings you to the monument to the Habsburg emperor Franz I. Its equestrian statue is missing: national feeling decreed that it should be banished to the National Museum. *Cross the square into Karolíny Světlé.*

2 Kaple Svatého Kříže

To your right is the Romanesque Kaple Svatého Kříže – the Rotunda of the Holy Cross.
A detour north brings you towards Anenské náměstí and the Divadlo Na zábradlí (theatre) where Václav Havel began his underground career in the 1960s as a stagehand. Turn right up Náprstkova, which brings you to Betlémské náměstí.

3 Betlémská Kaple

The square takes its name from the gabled Bethlehem Chapel (*see p38*), built by pre-Hussite reformists who had been denied the right to build a church – which is why a 'chapel' could accommodate 3,000! The Communists

encouraged the building of the present replica – apparently, Hussites were regarded as ideologically sound.
Turn left into Husova.

4 Husova

Shortly on the right is Kostel Svatého Jiljí (St Giles's Church). A touching fresco inside shows the hermit stricken by an arrow fired by an archer of the Visigoth king. The arrow had been destined for St Giles's pet deer, which looks surprised but unharmed.

A detour to your left along Řetězová takes you to Palác Jiřího z Poděbrad (House of the Lords of Kunštát – No. 3) which has a perfectly preserved Romanesque cellar (*see p122*). *Retrace your steps. Continue along Husova to the junction with souvenir-shop-packed Karlova. A detour right can be made here to the picturesque Malé náměstí; otherwise turn left into Karlova. Note the imposing Clam-Gallas Palace* (see p110) *just beyond the junction, with its portals supported by two Atlas figures.*
Cellar open: May–Oct, Tue–Sun 10am–noon, 1–6pm. Admission charge.

5 Karlova

Shortly on the right is the Klementinum (Clementinum) (*see p86*), a huge Jesuit seminary set up at the beginning of the Counter-Reformation. It was a centre of learning, as well as propaganda, and Johannes Kepler once scanned the night skies from its observatory.
Karlova opens into Křížovnické náměstí.

6 Křížovnické Náměstí

Knights of the Cross Square (*see p87*) has two churches – a Jesuit one, and the Franciscan Church of St Francis Seraphiscus (*see p39*) that belonged to the Knights of St John, guardians of the Judith Bridge (Charles Bridge's predecessor). By the bridge is a cast-iron statue of Charles IV.
From Křížovnické náměstí you can either stroll straight on to Malá Strana across the Karlův Most (Charles Bridge), or turn right and right again to follow Platneřská to Mariánské náměstí, and eventually Staroměstské náměstí. Alternatively, take tram 17 or 18, both of which run from the embankment nearby.

Statue of Charles IV overlooking the bridge that bears his name

Malá Strana

Malá Strana, the 'Lesser Quarter', is at once intimate and grandiose. Crowded with sumptuous Baroque palaces and churches, its narrow cobbled streets tail off into green garden-oases of silence, or snake towards the river through irregular medieval squares.

In 1257, the ambitious Přemysl Otakar II founded a 'New Town' in an area on the west bank of the Vltava hitherto consisting only of scattered communities. The latter included the Knights of St John, whose headquarters were beside the bridgehead of the Judith Bridge, as well as a few market traders, and the Jews of Újezd. The knights were allowed to stay, while the Jews and the other inhabitants were summarily evicted to make way for German merchants. New towns, directly dependent on royal privilege, were vital for the king's exchequer, and represented Otakar's attempt to outmanœuvre the Czech nobility, the latter having won the right to set their own level of taxation.

Otakar's 'New Town' was given the name 'Lesser Quarter' under Charles IV, who founded his own 'Nové Město' on the opposite bank of the river. The area was widely damaged in 1419 by the Hussites, and further devastated by the great fire of 1541. From the ashes rose Renaissance houses, together with a large Italian quarter that was established by the hundreds of Italian artisans attracted to Prague during the construction boom under Ferdinand and Rudolf (names like Vlašská (Italian) Street recall their presence).

Malá Strana acquired its present importance when Catholic nobles loyal to the Habsburgs were granted most of it in the 1620s, and built their fabulous palaces. The diminutive Baroque town – it encompasses a mere 60 hectares – has survived the turmoil of recent history almost unscathed. The main scenes of Miloš Forman's film *Amadeus*

THE WORLD OF JAN NERUDA

Nerudova, the street in Malá Strana named after the celebrated Czech writer and journalist Jan Neruda (1834–91), rises sharply from Malostranské náměstí towards the Hrad. Near its summit, at No. 47, is the house where Neruda was born, and the streets round about are the settings for his *Tales of the Lesser Quarter* (1878). No other writer evokes the day-to-day life of 19th-century Prague. Each story is a sharp vignette of late-Habsburg Prague.

Neruda, the son of a charwoman and a tobacconist, was in many ways typical of the milieu he describes. He fell foul of the conservative Czech nationalists, while his adherence to the 'Young Czech' cause made him suspect in the eyes of German officialdom. Deserted by friends and derided by his enemies, he died unjustly discredited and neglected.

Nerudova, where every door tells a tale

were set in virtually the same town as that which was visited by Mozart in 1787, when he stayed with his patron Count Thun, in what is now the British Embassy.

The Lesser Quarter's last great social upheaval was in 1948 when the Communists solved the housing shortage by dividing its palaces into apartments. Thereafter, the world's potentially most glamorous council houses slowly decayed for 40 years. After the restitution law of 1990, many have been taken over by private concerns and have been exquisitely renovated. *Malá Strana. Trams: 12, 18, 22, & 23 to Malostranské náměstí. Metro: to Malostranská.*

Malá Strana – a bird's-eye view

Walk: Malá Strana

This walk covers many of the most interesting sights of the Malá Strana (Lesser Quarter). The nobles built their great palaces here to be close to (or, in Wallenstein's case, to rival) the Royal Court of Hradčany.

Allow 2 hours.

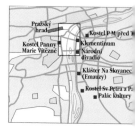

Begin at the Malostranská metro station (also the tram stop for Nos 12, 22, & 23), and turn left into Valdštejnská.

1 Valdštejnská

The street is filled with the palatial residences of the German nobility imported by the Habsburgs. The Valdštejnsky palác (Wallenstein Palace)

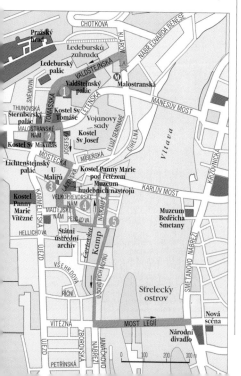

occupies the entire east side of Valdštejnské náměstí at the end of the street. Albrecht von Waldstein (Wallenstein to the English) was the greatest imperial commander in the Thirty Years War. His vaulting ambition proved his downfall: Emperor Ferdinand had him assassinated when he set his sights on becoming king of Bohemia. *From Valdštejnské náměstí continue into Tomášská and Malostranské náměstí (see pp94–5).*

2 Malostranské Náměstí

Malostranské náměstí (Lesser Quarter Square) manages to be both noble and intimate. The whole of the west side is occupied by the Lichtenstejnský palác (Liechtenstein Palace), home of the Liechtenstein who condemned the Protestant leaders to death in 1621, while in the Smiřický Palace to the north the plot was hatched that led to the defenestration of Ferdinand's Catholic councillors in 1618. Lording over these webs of intrigue is the Baroque **Kostel Svatého Mikuláše** (St Nicholas Church – *see pp94–5*), the greatest masterwork in Prague of the Dientzenhofers, father and son. *Walk east along Letenská, turning immediately right into Josefská, and* *passing the Kostel svatého Josef (St Joseph Church) with its narrow, Dutch-type façade. Turn left into Mostecká (always awash with tourists heading for the Karlův most – Charles Bridge), and then right into Lázeňská.*

3 Lázeňská

A few minutes on foot brings you to the area associated with the Maltese Knights (of the Order of St John), as recalled in the names of its two diminutive and picturesque squares: Maltézské náměstí (Maltese Square), and Velkopřevorské náměstí (Grand Prior's Square). A relic of their function as keepers of the first bridge across the Vltava is the chain hung above the high altar of their church, Kostel Panny Marie pod řetězem (Church of Our Lady below the Chain, accessible for Sunday mass at 10.30am, held in French). At No. 11 Maltese Square is the elegant little U Malíru (Painters' Tavern), now an exorbitantly expensive French restaurant.

Continue to the adjoining Velkopřevorské náměstí (Grand Prior's Square).

4 Velkopřevorské Náměstí

The Palace of the Grand Prior used to host the Muzeum Hudebních nastrojů (Musical Instruments Museum). A back wall has become an unofficial shrine to John Lennon, with graffiti portraits making him look a bit like a Byzantine saint.

Retrace your steps to Maltézské náměstí and enter Nosticova. Turn left on Pelclova and cross the bridge to Kampa Island.

5 Kampa Island

The bridge spans the Čertovka, or Devil's Stream, named after the tricky sprite thought to inhabit it (or possibly just an abusive reference to a famously grumpy local washerwoman – opinions differ).

It is worth taking a turn round the delightful 'island' and perhaps stopping for a drink at one of the pavement cafés below Charles Bridge on Na Kampe, where there are also a few good souvenir shops.

Leave Kampa by the southern end and climb up on to most Legií (the Bridge of the Legions). On the far side are the Národní divadlo (National Theatre) and tram stops.

The serene beauty of the streets on Kampa Island as seen from the Charles Bridge

Malostranské Náměstí

Once the outer bailey of the Prague castle, the Lesser
Quarter Square became the focus of the small town
founded by Otakar II in 1257. In the Middle Ages a
Romanesque rotunda dedicated to St Wenceslas stood in
the middle of it, along with a pillory and a gallows. The
Town Hall was established in the 15th century and later a
parish church of St Nicholas (Kostel Sv Mikuláše) was
built, dividing the upper and lower halves of the square.

Watch the world go by
outside the Town Hall

The Lower Square

Gothic, Renaissance, and Baroque
elements mingle gracefully in the lower
part of the square. To the west it is
closed by the rear walls of St Nicholas
and the former Jesuit College. In front
of these is the Rococo Grömling Palace
(built by Josef Jäger in 1773); the
Radetzky Café (named after the Austrian
general who put down the Italian
rebellion against the Habsburgs in 1848)
was opened on the ground floor, and
became a haunt of the Prague literati,
including Kafka, Brod, and Werfel. The
name 'Radetzky' did not survive the rise
of Czech nationalism – the café is now
the Malostranská kavárna (currently
closed for renovation).

On the east side of the square, at
No. 21, is the former Town Hall
(Malostranská radnice). It was here that
Protestant groups hammered out the
Bohemian Confession of 1575 that
guaranteed the freedom of religion.

On the north side of the Lower
Square are the Sternberg Palace (No.
15), where the great fire of 1541 broke
out, and the Smiřický palác (No. 18),
where the dissident Czech nobles plotted
the overthrow of Ferdinand II's hated
Catholic councillors on 22 May 1618.
On the following day, they matched
words by deeds by throwing the
councillors out of the windows of the
Bohemian Chancellery (the third
defenestration of Prague).

The Upper Square

At the centre of the square is Giovanni
Alliprandi's Plague Column (1715). The
whole of the west side is occupied by
the Liechtenstein Palace, whose Neo-
Classical façade dates to 1791. The
Liechtensteins lost their Czech
possessions (about 10 times the size of
the present Grand Duchy) in 1918; the
restitution law passed after the Velvet
Revolution only covered what had been
grabbed by the state after 1948, or they
could have received chunks of the Czech
Republic.

Kostel Sv Mikuláše
(Basilica of St Nicholas)

This beautiful basilica, opposite the
Liechtenstein Palace, is regarded by

many as the finest church in Prague, if not in Central Europe. Christoph Dientzenhofer, commissioned by the Jesuits, built the elegant façade (1710) and also completed the nave, the side-chapels, and the galleries before his death in 1722. His son Kilián Ignác built the choir and the ambitious dome (1752); the townspeople refused to enter the church until a commission of experts had pronounced it safe.

An outstanding feature of the interior is Lukáš Kracker's (1,500sq m) illusionist fresco on the ceiling of the nave, showing the Apotheosis of St Nicholas. The outsized statues of the early fathers of the church under the cupola are by Ignaz Platzer, who also sculpted that of St Nicholas above the high altar. The superb Rococo pulpit (1765) by Richard and Peter Práchner is decorated with allegories of Faith, Hope, and Charity; rather oddly juxtaposed is a scene of John the Baptist being beheaded. The splendour of the basilica makes a visit one of the most moving experiences.

Open: 9am–5pm. Admission charge. Trams: 12, 22, & 23 to Malostranské náměstí. Metro: Malostranská.

High Baroque sculpture inside the Basilica of St Nicholas

Museum interior

Museums

Although Prague has a clutch of museums covering natural history, art, and geology, its best are the peculiar but elegant Mucha Museum, the Museum of Flying, and the Museum of Toys.

The following selective list covers those of Prague's remaining minor museums that are likely to be of interest to the casual visitor.

Franz Kafka Permanent Exhibition
Kafka's life and works are shown in words and pictures.
U Radnice 5, just off Staroměstské náměstí. Open: Tue–Sun 10am–5pm, Sat 10am–6pm. Tram & metro: to Staroměstská. The bookshop is well worth a visit.

Letecké Muzeum Kbely (Museum of Flying)
Some 80 of the 200 aeroplanes in this museum are on display. The capsule in which the first Czech cosmonaut landed back on earth (1978) may also be seen, and there is extensive information on the former Czechoslovakia's participation in space research.
Kbely airport (Prague 9). Open: 1 May– 30 Oct, Tue–Thu, Sat & Sun 10am–6pm. Admission charge. Metro: z B to Českomoravská, then buses 185 & 259 to Letecké.

Lobkowicz Palác Narodni Historicke Muzeum (Lobkowicz Palace National History Museum)
A visit to this museum is best combined with a tour of Castle Hill. Exhibits include copies of the Bohemian Crown Jewels, and St Wenceslas's word, together with material relating to the Hussite wars and the Battle of the White Mountain.
Jiřská 3, Hradčany. Open: Tue–Sun 9am–5pm. Admission charge. Trams: 22 or 23 to Pražský hrad. Metro: to Malostranská.

Náprstkovo Muzeum (Náprstek Museum)
The museum contains artefacts from Native American, Oceanian, African, and Asian cultures.
Betlémské náměstí 1, Praha 1. Open: Tue–Sun 9am–noon, 12.45–5.30pm. Admission charge. Every first Fri in the month free. Trams: 6, 9, 18, & 22 to Národní divadlo. Metro: to Národní třída.

Muzeum Poštovní Známky (Postage Stamp Museum)
This rather charming and little-frequented museum has a stamp collection on the ground floor and some homely prints upstairs demonstrating that a postman's lot is not necessarily a happy one. It covers Czechoslovak and European stamps, as well as stamps of the Czech Republic.

Váurův dům, Nové mlýny 2.
Open: Tue–Sun 9am–5pm. Admission
charge. Trams: 5, 14, & 26 to Revolucní.

Uměleckoprůmyslové Muzeum (Museum of Decorative Arts)

Only a tiny proportion of the museum's vast horde of Renaissance to 19th-century treasures is on permanent display. A great deal of that is furniture, including some fine escritoires, cabinets, and clocks. The main focus is on 16th-to 19th-century European and Czech handicrafts, including ceramics, textiles, glass, fashion items, and metalwork. A selection of applied art is also shown at the Tyršovo Museum.
Ulice 17, listopadu 2. Open: Tue–Sun
10am–6pm. Admission charge.

Trams: 17 & 18.
Metro: to Staroměstská.

Vojenské Muzeum (Army Museum)

Formerly the Museum of the Resistance and the Czechoslovak Army, this has now been revamped to make it more informative than its predecessor. Topics covered include the story of the Czech Legions in World War I, and the assassination of the Nazi 'Reichs-protektor' Richard Heydrich during World War II *(see p42 & p142).*
U Památníku 2, Žižkov. Open: May–Oct,
Tue–Sun 10am–6pm; Nov–Apr, Mon–Fri
8.30am–5pm. Admission charge.
Buses: 133 & 207 to Pod památníkem.
Metro: to Florenc.

Lobkowicz palace houses the National History Museum

Neo-Renaissance façade of the National Theatre

Muzeum Alfons Mucha

A superb exhibition of the works of Alfons Mucha – and a good gift shop with fine Mucha posters.

Panská 7, Nové město. Open: daily 10am–6pm. Free admission.
Metro: Muzeum or Mistek.

Muzeum Policie (Police Museum)

Exhibits the history of the Czech (and Czechoslovak) police forces. There are also catchy displays on criminology and specific crimes, weapons, forensic sources, and the like.

Ke Karlovu 1, Prague 2. Open: Tue–Sun 10am–5pm. Admission charge.
Metro: IP Pavlova.

Muzeum Městské Hromadné Dopravy (City Transport Museum)

Houses a collection of historic vehicles, from 1886 to the present day.

Patočkova 4, Prague 6. Open: Apr–Nov, Sat–Sun & on holidays 9am–5pm; by appointment in winter (Dec–Mar).
Tel: (02) 312 3349.

Muzeum Hraček (Toy Museum)

The second-largest collection of toys in the world, in the beautiful Supreme Burgrave's house, this includes ancient as well as modern toys and games, Czech tin and wood toys.

Jířska, the Prague Castle. Open: daily 9.30am–5pm. Trams: 22 & 23.

Národní Divadlo (National Theatre)
František Palacký was the moving spirit behind the founding of the National Theatre. Prague until then had only German theatres that sometimes staged Czech plays. Josef Zítek's building was destroyed by fire even before it was officially opened; it was rebuilt between 1881 and 1883 by his pupil, Josef Schulz, who preserved his Neo-Renaissance design. It is lavishly decorated inside with allegorical and historical themes by leading artists of the time. The New Scene, a 1983 extension, was described by a writer as a 'translucent honeycomb'. *Národní třída 2. Tel: (02) 2490 1448.*

Performances usually begin at 7pm. Trams: 6, 9, 17, 18, 22, & 51 to Národní Divadlo.

Národní Technicke Muzeum (National Technical Museum)
A marvellous display of historic transport, from imperial railway carriages to early sports cars and aeroplanes. Space is also devoted to chronography, photography, astronomy, mining, and much else.
Kostelní 42, Letná, Prague 7.
Open: Tue–Sun 9am–5pm.
Admission charge. Trams: 1, 8, 25, & 26 to Letenské náměstí.

Early motorised vehicles on display at the National Technical Museum

On a grand scale – the National Museum

Muzeum Hlavního Města Prahy
(Museum of the City of Prague)

This museum contains substantial archaeological finds from the earliest times, plus impressive statuary and sculpture, ranging from a Gothic Madonna of 1383 to a fine bronze of Hercules by Adrian de Vries. The Baroque wood sculptures are by the finest Bohemian masters, including Jan Bendl, Ferdinand Brokoff, and Matthias Braun.

A curiosity is Antonín Langweil's model of historic Prague, which took him eight years to make (1826–34). Some 2,228 buildings have been lovingly recreated on a scale of 1:423, giving a unique picture of the city in the early 19th century.

Na Poříčí 52. Open: Tue–Sun 9am–6pm. Admission charge. First Thu in every month is free (open 9am–8pm). Trams: 3, 8, & 24 to Florenc.

Národní Muzeum
(National Museum)

The original project for the National Museum united the aspirations of the Czech and German populations, but by the time the present heavy Neo-Renaissance building (the museum's third home) was completed in 1891, it had become a pugnaciously Czech affair. Inside are somewhat forbidding departments of zoology and botany,

archaeology, palaeontology, and mineralogy to wade through.

The focus of the building is the heroic marble **Pantheon.** It is a huge, richly decorated space under the cupola, with statues and busts of famous Czechs, and lunettes painted by František Ženíšek and Václav Brožík showing major events from the nation's past. Six over-lifesize statues are placed next to the pillars: four giants of Bohemia's past – Jan Hus, Jan Comenius, František Palacký, and Tomáš Masaryk – plus two comparative lightweights – Count Šternberk, the founder of the museum, and the writer, Jan Neruda.

Václavské náměstí 68.
Tel: (02) 2423 0485. Open: daily
10am–6pm (5pm Oct–Apr). Admission charge. Metro: to Museum.

Tomáš Garrigue Masaryk

In its short existence (1918–92), Czech-oslovakia produced two statesmen who won the respect of the world: Václav Havel and Tomáš Masaryk (1850–1937). Masaryk was of humble origin – an illegitimate child brought up by Slovak peasants. He rose to become a professor of philosophy and a Social Democratic MP in the Reichsrat (Parliament) of the Austro-Hungarian Empire. In exile during World War I, he laid the foundation of the new Czechoslovak Republic, which proved to be a model of stability and democracy under his presidency (1918–35), although emphatically a pan-Slavic nation rather than a more multi-cultural one.

A glorious celebration of Neo-Renaissance design – interior, National Museum

'What is life? An illusion, a shadow, a story . . .' wrote the 17th-century Spanish dramatist Calderón, a reflection which might well be applied to Prague's avant-garde illusionist theatres.

The cunning use of spectacle, illusion, and music has its roots at least as far back as the propagandist art and drama sponsored by the Jesuits in the Baroque age. Modern technology opened the way to a new form of multi-media spectacle first developed by Alfréd Redok in the 1950s. His Laterna Magika (Magic Lantern) shows made sophisticated use of lighting and film projection, and won world acclaim at the Brussels Expo of 1958. The idea has proved a runaway success at the box office. Its more or less imitative spin-offs

include Theatrum Novum, and the Laterna Animata.

The show is a mix of live acting and scenic *coups de théâtre* brought about by film or slide projection and dramatic lighting effects. The third ingredient is music. Particularly successful are reworked myths, such as that of the *Odyssey* in terms of 'the common dawn and early childhood of today's Europe'.

It has to be admitted that there are times when gimmickry overwhelms the drama. On the other hand, the criticism that Laterna Magika is merely a faked theatrical 'happening' put on for visitors misses the point. The shows are popular because they are exciting and brilliantly staged. These performances are a unique part of Prague's theatre culture.

Productions in the repertoire include *Magic Circus*, *The Minotaur*, *Odysseus*,

The Magic Lantern is an experience unique to Prague

and *Carmina Burana*. The shows take place in the Nová Scéna of the National Theatre. For booking arrangements, *see pp152–3*.

Music Museums

Bertramka

This charming 17th-century villa (and gardens), which houses the memorial to Wolfgang Mozart and Mr & Mrs Dušek, is named after its second owner, František Bertram. However, it owes its fame to the fact that Mozart stayed here with his friends Josefa Dušková, the opera singer, and her composer husband, František. Mozart was allegedly locked into one of the rooms until he had completed a long-promised aria for Josefa, and may also have completed the overture to *Don Giovanni* here.

There is an exhibition of the composer's life and work in the villa, and a bust of him by Tomáš Seidan in the garden. Charming concerts of Mozart arias and other works are held in the villa and in the gardens in summer.

Mozartova 169, Smíchov. Open: daily 9.30am–6pm (5pm in winter). Admission charge. Trams: 4, 6, 7, & 9 to Bertramka. Metro: (line B) to Anděl, and a 1.5km walk.

Statue of Bedřich Smetana

MOZART IN PRAGUE

Mozart arrived for his second visit to Prague in the autumn of 1787 with a new opera under his arm. *The Seraglio* and *The Marriage of Figaro* had already brought him fame with the musically sophisticated Prague public; *Don Giovanni*, premiered on 29 October at the Estates Theatre (*see* p131.), was an even greater triumph. *La Clemenza di Tito*, premiered in the autumn of 1791, was considered old-fashioned and was not well received. Mozart died two months later on 5 December in Vienna, virtually unmourned by his compatriots. However, Prague staged a grand memorial service for him on 14 December in the Kostel Sv Mikuláše (St Nicholas Church) of the Lesser Quarter. The church, with a capacity of 4,000 people, was filled to overflowing and carriages blocked the surrounding streets. Josefa Dušková led the requiem singers.

The Dvořák Museum, housed in a Baroque villa designed by Kilián Dientzenhofer

Muzeum Antonína Dvořáka (Antonín Dvořák Museum – Vila Amerika)

The name of this gem of a Baroque villa, built by Kilián Ignác Dientzenhofer, and with statues from Matthias Braun's workshop, refers to a hotel that used to stand nearby, not to Dvořák's famous *New World Symphony*.

The Dvořák collection includes musical scores and correspondence. One of the greatest of the 19th-century Romantic composers, Antonín Dvořák (1841–1904) drew much inspiration from Czech folk music.

Ke Karlovu 20. Open: Tue–Sun 10am–5pm. Admission charge. Trams: 4, 6, 10, 16, 22, & 23. Metro: to IP Pavlova.

Muzeum Bedřicha Smetany (Bedřich Smetana Museum)

A modern statue of the great Czech composer sitting under a willow with his back to his beloved Vltava, is almost the only item of note in this otherwise undistinguished museum on the life and works of Smetana (1824–84). Smetana composed the music most closely identified with the patriotic aspirations of Bohemia. His best known works are *The Bartered Bride* and *Dalibor*, and his tone poem *My Country* contains a famous passage beautifully evoking the surging waters of the Vltava.

Novotného lávka 1. Open: daily 10am–5pm. Closed: Tue. Admission charge. Trams: 17 & 18 to Karlovy lázně. Metro: to Staroměstská.

Musical Prague

'Music', according to an old Prague saying, 'was born of necessity and became a necessity.' It was in the 17th century, however, that musical culture truly burgeoned in Bohemia and Moravia, particularly in the court of Rudolf II and under the influence of Prince-Bishop Karl Liechtenstein-Kastelcorn of Olomone. By the 18th century, Czech composers were famous all over Europe, including Zelenka, Mysliveček, Vranický, and Koželuh.

Prague audiences are traditionally more musically literate than elsewhere. As early as the 1720s, the public could buy cheap seats in private theatres, where censorship was also lax compared with the stiff court opera in Vienna. Thus, the people of Prague understood and loved the music of Mozart at a time when Vienna turned its back on him. Nowadays, Prague's year-round music festivals, most famously the international Prague Spring Music Festival (12 May–3 June), attract music-lovers from all over the world.

Throughout the year churches, former convents, and Baroque palaces ring to the sound of sacred and profane harmonies. The giants of Czech music, Bedřich Smetana (1824–84), Antonín Dvořák (1841–1904), and the Moravian Leoš Janáček (1854–1938), tend to dominate the symphony programmes. Opera and symphony concerts are held in the great auditoria built during the late 19th-century boom of patriotic culture: the National Theatre (Národní Divadlo, 1881), the Rudolfinum (1884),

and the Municipal House (Obecní Dům, 1911); but many delightful works by minor composers of the Czech Baroque are played in such romantic settings as Bazilika Svatého Jiří (St George's Basilica) on Castle Hill.

In the 18th century the English musicologist, Charles Burney, gave Prague the title of 'The Music Conservatory of Europe'. Were he to come back now, he would see no reason to change his opinion. Hurrying figures with

cello cases are still to be seen on the streets, and on languid summer afternoons melodious strains waft from many an open window.

From classical to pop, Prague caters to all musical tastes

Stálé Expozice Národní Galerie
National Gallery Collections

Exhibit at the St George's Convent

Anežský Klášter
(St Agnes' Convent)
Czech Art of the 19th Century

The cloister and convent feature Czech
Gothic art, and also house long-term
but temporary exhibitions of Czech art
and sculpture (*see pp26–7*).
*U Milosrdných 17. Tel: (02) 2481 0628.
Open: Tue–Sun 10am–6pm. Admission
charge. Metro: to Staroměstská or
Náměstí Republiky, then trams 5, 14, or
26 to Révoluční.*

Klášter Sv Jiří Na Pražském Hradě
(St George's Convent at Prague
Castle)
Collection of Old Bohemian Art

The gallery is divided into two sections:
Gothic art in the basement and at
ground-floor level, Baroque works on
the first floor. Among the former are
fine examples of International Gothic or
'Beautiful Style'. One of the earliest free-
standing sculptures (1373) is the bronze
St George and the Dragon.

High points are the nine-panelled
altarpiece from the Cistercian monastery
at Vyssí Brod, and paintings of saints by
Master Theodoric. Arresting Baroque
works include Bartolomaeus Spranger's
The Risen Christ, and sculptures by
Maximilian Brokoff and Matthias
Braun, in particular the latter's sculpture
of St Jude.
*Jiřské náměstí 33. Hradčany. Tel: (02)
5732 0889. Open: Tue–Sun 10am–6pm.
Admission charge. Trams: 22 or 23 to
Pražský hrad. Metro: to Malostranská.*

Šternberský Palác (Sternberg Palace)
**Old European Art, French 19th- and
20th-century Art**

Albrecht Dürer's *The Feast of the Rose
Garlands* is the gallery's most celebrated
possession, which also features early
European art of the 14th and 15th
centuries, Dutch paintings of the 15th
century, Roman schools of the 17th and
18th centuries, Flemish 17th-century
paintings, and German and Austrian
paintings of the 15th–18th centuries.
Among these are some fine works by
Rembrandt, Holbein, Veneto, Rubens,
and Van Dyck.
*Hradčanské náměstí 15. Tel: 2051 4598.
Open: Tue–Sun 10am–6pm. Admission*

charge. Trams: 22 or 23 to Pražský hrad. Metro: to Malostranská.

Zámek Zbraslav (Zbraslav Castle)
Collection of 19th- and 20th-century Czech Sculpture

This former monastery where non-European works of art are housed is well worth the trek. It also holds temporary exhibitions.

Zbraslav nad Vltavou, Prague V. Tel: (02) 5792 0481. Open: Tue–Sun 10am–6pm. Closed: Nov–Apr. Admission charge. Metro: (line B) to Smíchovské nádraží, then buses 129, 241, 243, or 255 to Zbraslavské náměstí.

Veletržní Palác
(Palace of Fairs)

Designed for the Prague Trade Fair of 1928, this huge glass-fronted building was described by Le Corbusier, the famous 20th-century architect, as 'breathtaking'. Among the many outstanding collections of 19th- and 20th-century Czech and European art are *Green Rye* by Van Gogh (1889), *Two Women Among the Flowers* by Monet (1875), and one of Gauguin's Tahiti paintings, *Flight* (1902). There are works

by Picasso, Braque, Chagall, Dufy, Derain, and Vlaminck. Sculptures include works by Rodin and Henri Laurens.

Dukelských hrdinů 47. Tel: (02) 2430 1175. Open: Tue–Sun 10am–6pm, Thu until 9pm. Admission charge. Trams: 5 & 12.

Sternberg Palace houses art treasures of the 14th–18th centuries

Inside Clam-Gallas Palace

Palaces

The majority of Prague's noble palaces are today occupied by government institutions, museums, or embassies. Most are the product of the building boom in Baroque times.

After the Battle of the White Mountain in 1620, German aristocrats and war profiteers loyal to the Habsburgs took over property that had belonged to the now-exiled Bohemian nobility, or bought up land at depressed prices. The most spectacular example of megalomaniac building from this period is the huge Valdštejnský Palác (Wallenstein Palace) in Malá Strana (*see pp112–13*); to make way for it 23 houses, three gardens, and a brickworks were demolished.

A Baroque palace was designed to display its owner's wealth and importance – the secular equivalent of Baroque church architecture with its fabulous ornamentation. This period of ostentatious noble display lasted until the second half of the 18th century, when centralising reforms under Maria Theresa and Joseph II reduced the power and importance of the aristocracy. Few palaces were built after about 1750, although a number of existing ones were rebuilt or refurbished to reflect contemporary taste.

The palaces listed below have been chosen for their aesthetic or historical interest. The list excludes those described in the contexts of Hradčanské náměstí (*see pp68–9*), Malostranské náměstí (*see pp94–5*), and Staroměstské náměstí (*see pp124–7*).

Clam-Gallasovský Palác (Clam-Gallas Palace)

The palace was built between 1713 and 1719 by Domenico Canevalle to a design by the great Viennese architect Johann Bernhard Fischer von Erlach. For such a noble building it may seem rather cramped in its surroundings on Husova. Indeed, the owner had assumed that he would be able to demolish the block opposite so that his palace would look on to a square. Not surprisingly, the residents had other ideas, so that a mortified Count Gallas had to be content with what he had.

Notable are the Atlas figures of the two doorways, the work of Matthias Braun, who also made the rest of the sculptural decoration. Inside there is a grand staircase with stucco by Santo Rossi, and above it a fresco (*The Triumph of Apollo*) by Carlo Carlone. The city archives are now housed in the palace, which means that you can usually wander in to have a look. *Husova ulice 20, Staré Město. The palace is open for researchers in the city archives. Trams: 17 & 18 to Staroměstská.*

Černínský Palác (Černín Palace)

Four generations of Černíns and as many architects worked on this enormous palace (its façade is 135m wide). Jan Černín, who conceived the project, was ambassador in Venice, where he is said to have persuaded Bernini to do the first sketch for the building. It was not completed until 1720. Since 1932 it has belonged to the Ministry of Foreign Affairs. In 1948 Jan Masaryk, the only non-Communist in the government, mysteriously 'fell' to his death from its upper floor – possibly the last Prague defenestration.

Loretánské náměstí 5, Hradčany. The palace is not open to the public.
Trams: 22 or 23 to Památník písemnictví.

Lobkowický Palác (Lobkowicz Palace)

The powerful Lobkowicz family ended up with no less than three palaces in Prague, of which this is the most aesthetic – a masterwork by Giovanni Alliprandi (1707), with a further storey added in 1769 by Ignaz Palliardi.

The best view of its Baroque splendour is from the far side of the English landscape garden at the rear (the palace is now the German embassy, but access to the garden is sometimes possible). David Černý's bizarre sculpture of a gold-painted Trabant bearing the title *Quo Vadis?* is here, commemorating the time in 1989 when hundreds of East Germans occupied the embassy grounds, demanding West German citizenship.

Vlašská ulice 19, Malá Strana. Open: only to those on embassy business. Trams: 12, 22, & 23 to Malostranské náměstí.

The Czech Foreign Ministry functions from the Černín Palace

Morzinský Palác (Morzin Palace)

A striking feature of the Morzin Palace's façade is the two muscle-bound figures of Moors supporting the balcony. This is a reference to the family name, Morzin – 'Moor' in Czech. The architect, Giovanni Santini-Aichel, created the palace out of three older houses in 1714. All the sculptural decoration is by Ferdinand Brokoff: above the two side doorways are allegories of *Day* and *Night*, while the *Four Corners of the World* are represented on the roof. The building is now occupied by the Romanian embassy.

Nerudova ulice 5, Malá Strana. Open: only to those on embassy business. Trams: 12, 22, & 23 to Malostranské náměstí.

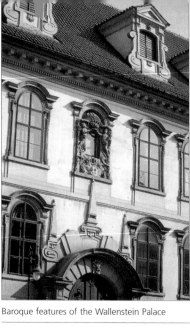
Baroque features of the Wallenstein Palace

Nostickův Palác (Nostic Palace)

The Nostic family, great patrons and collectors of art in the 17th century, commissioned Francesco Caratti to build this sumptuous palace in 1658. Additions and alterations were made by Giovanni Santini-Aichel in the 18th century; Ferdinand Brokoff added statues of Roman emperors. The Nostic family built up their own picture gallery, and a library which still survives. The building is now shared between the Dutch embassy and the Ministry of Education. Scenes from the film *Amadeus* were shot in the palace's Baroque interiors.

Maltézské náměstí 1, Malá Strana. Scholars may visit the library. Trams: 12, 22, & 23 to Hellichova.

Thun-Hohenstejnský Palác (Thun-Hohenstein Palace)

This vast palace is a good example of buildings in Malá Strana whereby rich owners of small plots of land relentlessly extended their residences by buying up their less wealthy neighbours. The present building dates from 1726, and was designed by Giovanni Santini-Aichel. The eagles with outstretched wings over the entrance (by Matthias Braun) are the heraldic birds of the Kolowrat family, who originally built the palace. The Thun-Hohensteins inherited it only in 1768. The Italian embassy now occupies the building.

Nerudova ulice 20, Malá Strana. Open: only to those on embassy business. Trams: 12, 22, & 23 to Malostranské náměstí.

Valdštejnský Palác (Wallenstein Palace)

Albrecht von Waldstein (in English 'Wallenstein') was one of the great opportunists of history. Although he came of Protestant stock, he served the Habsburgs in the Thirty Years War, rising swiftly to become Commander of the Imperial Armies. Having amassed a gigantic fortune, he decided to build the grandest palace in Prague, and demolished a large slice of the Lesser Quarter to do so. The resulting palace remained in the hands of the Wallenstein family until 1945.

The Wallenstein Palace was built between 1624 and 1630 to plans by Andrea Spezza. It encompassed five courtyards and a spectacular garden, and was surrounded by a high wall. The most attractive part of the whole complex is the graceful Renaissance loggia at the west end of the garden, built by Giovanni Pieroni. It is decorated with stucco and frescoes depicting the Trojan War by Baccio Bianco. Bianco also pandered to Wallenstein's taste for self-glorification by painting a fresco inside the palace showing him as the god Mars gliding above the clouds in his victory chariot.

The building's main façade occupies a whole side of Valdštejnské náměstí, but its serried banks of windows and three storeys are more formidable than pleasing. The overall design, which mingles late-Renaissance and early-Baroque features, seldom achieves the harmonious elegance of later Baroque architecture in Prague.

Niccolò Sebregondi laid out the gardens, at the far end of which is a large Baroque riding school. The garden boasts bronzes by the Dutch artist Adam de Vries, and has a grotto with tufa stalactites at its north end.

The palace belongs to the Ministry of Culture, and contains the Jan Comenius Pedagogical Museum.
Valdštejnské náměstí 4, Malá Strana. Trams: 12, 22, 23, &18. Metro: to Malostranská.

Tranquillity reigns in the attractive gardens of the Wallenstein Palace

Patrician and Burgher Houses

In the Middle Ages, house owners in Prague began the practice of identifying their properties by means of ornamental symbols, wall paintings, or simply, everyday objects attached to the façade. Trade premises would also be appropriately decorated (for example, the violin-maker's house on Nerudova boasts a detailed relief of three violins; and above the door of a former tavern on Husova, two figures are shown carrying a vast bunch of grapes on a pole).

Before numbering was introduced, Prague houses were identified by picturesque signs

In the 18th century, Maria Theresa introduced the so-called *Conscriptions-nummern* (conscription numbers) for houses, not only to rationalise the addresses of city dwellers, but also to facilitate the systematic checking of army conscription lists.

Despite the introduction of house numbers, many picturesque signs still survive. Most date from Baroque times, although some go back even earlier. The houses described below (five out of many such) have retained their decorative idiosyncrasies. Only those that are restaurants or partly shops may be visited inside.

Rottův Dům (Rott House)
The cellars of this house still have their Gothic vaulting, and follow the foundations of a Romanesque dwelling on this site. In the 15th century, a printshop situated here produced Prague's first printed Bible in 1488. The present Neo-Renaissance aspect of the building is the result of alterations

made in 1890, when it was owned by an iron merchant named Rott (his name is blazoned across the façade). The front wall was painted with decorative foliage and vignettes by Mikoláš Aleš. Notable are the charming emblematic figures for agriculture and the crafts, whose iron tools were Rott's stock in trade.
Malé náměstí 3, Staré Město. Trams: 17 & 18. Metro: to Staroměstská.

U Dvou Zlatých Medvědů (At the Two Golden Bears)
The Renaissance portal of this house has been preserved, but otherwise its aspect is Neo-Classical, following rebuilding in 1800. Above the lintel are two stone bears (originally gilded). Animals (apparently often chosen at random) were popular motifs for house signs.
Kožná ulice 1, Staré Město. Metro: to Můstek.

U Samuela (At Samuels)
This originally Gothic, later 'Baroquised' house is situated in the pedestrian zone

just below Václavské náměstí (Wenceslas Square). It takes its name from the relief on the corner of the building that shows the biblical King David as a child being anointed as future leader of his people by the prophet Samuel.

Na můstku 4, Staré Město.
Metro: to Můstek.

U Tří Pštrosů
(At the Three Ostriches)

The sign for this house was an advertisement: the 17th-century owner traded in ostrich feathers! Baroque alterations to the building were made in 1657, when the gables were added. An Armenian named Deodatus Damajan may have founded Prague's first coffee-house here in the 18th century, and long before that there was a restaurant on the ground floor (as there still is). In 1976, a luxury hotel was added to the facilities.

Dražického náměstí 12. Malá Strana.
Trams: 12 & 22 to Malostranské náměstí.

U Zlatého Jelena
(At the Golden Stag)

The 'golden stag' here is a spectacular sculptural group above the portals, the work of Ferdinand Brokoff. It shows St Hubert kneeling before an amiable-looking deer: according to legend, St Hubert went hunting on Good Friday and encountered a stag with a golden crucifix lodged in its antlers. This was taken as a warning that he should repent his sacrilegious disregard of a holy day. The Baroque house was built by Kilián Ignác Dientzenhofer in 1726.

Tomášská ulice 4, Malá Strana.
Trams: 12 & 22 to Malostranské náměstí.
Metro: to Malostranská.

The front of the Rottův dům is decorated with murals and cartoons by Mikoláš Aleš

Baroque Prague

In the 17th and 18th centuries, the face of Prague changed, reflecting the triumph of the Habsburg dynasty, and of Catholicism in Bohemia. The Baroque style was the official stamp placed on the city by the victors in the struggle for the nation's body and soul.

Baroque architecture still dominates the historic areas of Prague, especially Malá Strana and Hradčanské náměstí. Here the nobility built their fabulous palaces, competing with each other and the emperor in displays of wealth and splendour. Baroque forms were imported from Italy, and at first, chiefly Italian architects were employed.

The Catholic nobility's power and privilege were underlined by the allegorical sculptures of mythological heroes that ornamented the façades and gardens of their palaces. Atlas figures support their splendid entrances, and representations

of Hercules triumphant against his foes embellish many stairways or avenues.

Similarly, the magnificent Baroque churches are symbols of the Catholic church's triumphant Counter-Reformation that followed the defeat of the Protestant cause at the Battle of the White Mountain in 1620.

Prague produced some great Baroque masters, although they were nearly all of foreign origin (František Kaňka is one notable exception). Christoph Dientzenhofer and his son Kilián Ignác were Germans, Jean-Baptiste Mathey came from France, and Giovanni Santini-Aichel from Italy. The prolific Dientzenhofers built the loveliest of Prague's Baroque churches – including the two St Nicholases on Malostranské náměstí and Staroměstské náměstí – as well as many secular buildings. Catholic

orders (especially the Jesuits) poured money into religious architecture, and dozens of Gothic churches up and down the land were 'Baroquised'.

Cupolas, towers, terraced gardens, pathos-ridden gesticulating statues – all these conjure a vision of a city once suffused with religious fervour, but which was, simultaneously, the playground of mighty princes.

Prague's houses and churches are rich in Baroque decoration. Facing page below: Baroque doorways – a statement of power

Náměstí Jana Palacha (Jan Palach Square)

The square commemorates Jan Palach, the student who burned himself to death on Wenceslas Square in the protests following the Soviet invasion of 1968. Palach was a 21-year-old student at the Faculty of Philosophy, which runs along one side of the square. His bust has been erected on the corner of the faculty building.
Trams: 17 & 18.
Metro: to Staroměstská.

Petřín (Petřín Hill)

Petřín Hill, an eastern outrider of the White Mountain, was made into a public park in the 19th century. In 1901, it was linked to the Kinsky Gardens by a gap in the Hunger Wall.

According to the 11th-century chronicler, Cosmas of Prague, it derives its name from the Latin *petrus* ('stone'); the city did once get most of its building material from here. Later, it was covered with vineyards, and is today a tranquil wooded park with winding paths, that attracts Praguers of all ages to walk here in spring when its orchards are in blossom.

Lanová Dráha (Funicular Railway)

The funicular carries you up to the sights of Petřín. On the way it stops at the Nebozízek café and restaurant, which takes its name from the vineyard originally here; its terrace offers good views of the city, and the restaurant serves excellent game dishes.
Open: daily 9.15am–8.45pm. Trams: 6, 9, 12, 22, & 23 to Újezd. Small charge (one 15-minute public transport ticket).

The Calvary Chapel nestles among the wooded slopes of Petřín Hill

Petřínská Rozhledna (Petřín Tower)

Atop the hill is a scaled-down copy of the Eiffel Tower in Paris, made for the Prague Industrial Exhibition of 1891. There are 299 steps to the viewing platform, and no lift, but the view is worth it – you can see some Czech mountain ranges in Krkonoše on a clear day.
Open: Jun–Oct 10am–6pm.
Admission charge.

Kostel Sv Vavřince na Petříne (The Church of St Lawrence on Petřín)

The Germans call Petřín 'Laurenziberg' after the man to whom this church is dedicated, whose Romanesque forebear is first mentioned in records of 1135. Kilián Ignác Dientzenhofer and Ignác Palliardi rebuilt it in Baroque style between 1735 and 1770. St Adalbert, the martyred 10th-century bishop of

Prague, is commemorated by a statue, an altar painting, and a ceiling fresco depicting him founding the church.

Nearby are stations of the cross, culminating in a Calvary Chapel with 19th-century sgraffiti by Mikuláš Aleš.

Bludiště
(The 'Mirror Maze')

An odd-looking pavilion near St Lawrence contains a labyrinth of mirrors. At the end of this is a diorama of Prague students resisting the onslaught of the Swedes in the invasion of 1648.

Open: Apr–Aug 9am–7pm, Sep–Oct 10am–6pm, Nov–Mar 10am–5pm, weekends only. Admission charge.

Hvězdárna Hlavního Města
(The People's Observatory)

The Astronomical Institute of the Czech Academy of Sciences is based here, and amateurs are allowed to look through the telescopes. The most modern is a 40-cm Zeiss, but the older instruments, affectionately known as 'The King' and 'The Comet Finder', are still in use. *The Observatory's opening times are incredibly complicated. It is best to ring 2451 0709 if you want to visit.*

Hladová Zed (Hunger Wall)

Charles IV had this great fortification built between 1360 and 1362, supposedly as a job-creation scheme for the starving unemployed of the city (hence the name). The wall runs down the hill from the border of the gardens of Strahovský Klášter (Strahov Monastery) in the northwest to that of the Kinsky Garden in the southeast.

Access to Petřín Hill: by funicular from the station above Újezd (trams 12 & 22); from the gardens of Strahov Monastery (tram 22 to Památník písemnictví); from Vlašská ulice (trams 12 & 22 to Malostranské náměstí).

Jan Palach's sacrifice has not been forgotten

Obecní Dům

The Municipal House

Architecture was one of the expressions of the increasing self-confidence of the Czech nation which they achieved by the last decade of the 19th century. In Bohemia, 'municipal' or 'national' houses sprang up, combining representational, recreational, and social facilities.

Art Nouveau in the ascendant

Naturally, Prague had the biggest and best Municipal House; its full name – *Representační Dům Hlavního Města Praha* (the Central Representation House of the City of Prague) – indicates its aspirations. It was to be the focus of the Czech capital, celebrating the Czech people. It was here that MPs issued the Epiphany Declaration of January 1918, demanding the setting up of an independent Czechoslovak state.

The site chosen for this display of civic and national pride was very appropriate; it was to be built where the court of the Jagiello king had stood, next to the 'Powder Tower' (*see pp122–3*). When the tower was built in the 15th century, the municipality had financed that too, and the burghers had inscribed a declaration on it stressing that it was erected 'to the honour . . . of the citizens of the town'; their rulers were expected to get the message. The tower's main architect, Matěj Rejsek, has been remembered with a statue on the nearest corner of the Municipal House. A competition for the design was won by Antonín Balšánek and Osvald Polívka. Their project was realised in Art Nouveau style (*see pp30–31*) between 1905 and 1911. It was the most ambitious Art Nouveau building in the whole country, and is in superb condition, thanks to immaculate restoration in the 1990s.

The Exterior

The façade is a glorious clutter of glass ornament, wrought-iron railings, and theatrical statuary. It is topped by a glazed dome, beneath which a huge arched gable frames Karel Spillar's symbolic mosaic *Homage to Prague*.

The Interior

All the leading artists of the Czech Secession had a hand in the decoration of the marvellous interior. Immediately to your right is a vast French restaurant with lavish decor: ornamental stucco and huge gilt chandeliers set off the acres of mural with themes such as 'Hop Growing', 'Viticulture', or 'Prague Welcomes its Visitors'. Across the vestibule to the left is the equally ornate café, dominated at one end by a fountain with a nymph sculpted from Carrara marble by Josef Pekárek.

In the basement are a surprisingly cheap beer cellar and wine bar with artistic murals and ceramics.

First Floor

The focal point is the **Smetanova Síň** (Smetana Hall). Here, the composer Bedřich Smetana's emotionally charged symphonic poem *Má Vlast (My Country)* is performed at the beginning of the Prague Spring Festival (*see p154*). The sculptural groups flanking the stage represent Dvořák's *Bohemian Dances* and scenes from Smetana's opera *Vyšehrad*.

The most important of the other rooms is the **Sál Primátorský,** the circular mayoral hall decorated with paintings by Alfons Mucha, an artist who designed a pavilion for the Paris World Exhibition of 1900.

Also impressive is the **Rieger sál**, with Max Švabinský's large painted panels entitled *Prague Spring*.
Náměstí Republiky 5.
Metro: to Náměstí Republiky.

Glorious frescoes adorn both the façade and the interior of the Obecní dům

Palác Jiřího z Poděbrad (Poděbrad Palace)

Few remnants of Romanesque dwellings remain in Europe, but Prague has more than its fair share. The most striking is the Poděbrad Palace, the basement of which retains its original Romanesque cross-vaulting and fireplaces. What now appears to be the cellar was once the ground floor of the house, before street levels were raised during flood protection works in the second half of the 13th century.

The palace was built at the end of the 12th century or the beginning of the 13th for the Lords of Kunštát and Poděbrad. In 1406, according to the city records, the owner was Lord Boczko of Kunštát, the uncle of George of Poděbrad (*see box*), who inherited the building and lived here between 1453 and 1458.

In 1970 the restored palace was opened to the public. Inside it is a small display of ceramics, and an exhibit on the life of George of Poděbrad. *Řetězová ulice 3. Open: May–Oct, Tue–Sun 10am–noon, 1–6pm.*

Admission charge. Metro: to Můstek.

Letohrádek Portheimka (Portheimka Summer Palace)

The lightness and grace of this diminutive Baroque *Lustschloss* are a delight. The architect Kilián Ignác Dientzenhofer built it for his own family in 1729. Its present name recalls a 19th-century owner. An oval saloon with frescoed ceiling looks out on what was once a pleasant garden. It now houses a gallery, café, and local radio station for classical music.

Prague 5, Matoušova ulice 9, Smíchov. Tel: (02) 54 0651. Café open: 10am–10pm. Metro: to Anděl.

Prašná Brána (Powder Tower)

King Vladislav Jagiello laid the foundation stone for this huge gate-tower in 1475. It replaced an earlier gateway at the point where the trade from the east entered the city. The new fortification was modelled on the Staré Město tower at the end of the Charles Bridge (*see pp84–5*). For a while the king had his residence next door to it, but later, the hostility of

JIŘÍ Z PODĚBRAD (GEORGE OF PODĚBRAD) – KING OF BOHEMIA 1458–71

The followers of Jan Hus, the religious reformer, were divided between radical 'Táborites' and moderate Utraquists.

The greatest leader of the Utraquist faction was George Poděbrad, who became regent during the minority of King Ladislav. When the latter died in 1457, Poděbrad was elected king by the Bohemian Diet. To mark this event a chalice (the Utraquist symbol) was placed on the façade of the Týn Church (*see p126*).

The reign of George of Poděbrad marked the last, albeit glorious, phase of Hussite independence: the king withstood the machinations of the papacy and tried to unite the princes of Europe against increasing Turkish threat. He was the most able leader of his day, and is regarded as one of the greatest heroes of Bohemian history.

Detail of window, Portheimka

the Hussite burghers compelled him to retreat to the Hradčany.

In the 18th century the tower was used as a powder magazine, and was badly damaged when Frederick the Great attacked the city in 1757. Josef Mocker conscientiously 're-Gothicised' it in 1875, when the statues were placed on the façade.

The tower can be climbed by those prepared to negotiate the 186 steps for the view of Staré Město from the top. *Náměstí Republiky. Open: daily 10am–5pm (6pm in summer). Admission charge. Metro: to Náměstí Republiky.*

Architect Dientzenhofer built the splendid Baroque Portheimka for his family

Staroměstské Náměstí

Old Town Square

If Hradčany was the centre of royal authority in Prague, Staroměstské náměstí was the focus of people's power. John of Luxembourg first gave permission for a Town Hall to be built here in 1338, but an independent-minded municipality had existed long before that.

Old Town Hall

The square had been the focus of trade and exchange in the 12th and 13th centuries. Goods came in from the east through the customs house in Týn Court (*see p131*), and out on the ancient trade route that crossed the Vltava via the old Judith Bridge (*see p84*). Romanesque remains show the existence of a thriving community then. Most of these buildings were rebuilt in the Gothic style, later receiving a Baroque or Renaissance cladding.

Staroměstské náměstí has always been at the heart of Czech identity. After the first defenestration of Prague in 1419 (*see p45*), the ringleader, Jan Želivský, was executed on the square. The rebellious Protestant nobles met the same fate after the Battle of the White Mountain (1620); they are recalled by 27 white crosses set in the paving in front of the Town Hall. The Hussites (*see p38*) had their hour of glory when their candidate, George of Poděbrad, was elected king in the town hall in 1458. Jan Hus himself is honoured with a massive symbolic statue.

In modern times Staroměstské náměstí has again been the setting where history was made. It saw the jubilation that marked the beginning of Communist rule in 1948, the furious protest at its continuing usurpation of power in 1968, and joy at its demise in 1989. It is also the focal point for demonstrations and celebrations today, such as the frequent Czech ice-hockey victories in the world championships, broadcast live in the square.

Staroměstská Radnice (Old Town Hall)

At the southwest corner is the Old Town Hall, which has reached its present proportions by steadily swallowing up neighbouring buildings between the 14th and 19th centuries. In the Great Hall are Václav Brožík's heroic representations of the *Election of George of Poděbrad* and *Jan Hus before the Council of Constance,* complementing the patriotic mosaics in the entrance hall. On the southern façade is the famous **Orloj** (astronomical clock). On the hour, every hour, Christ and the 12 apostles emerge, and the skeleton of Death tolls a bell with one hand while holding a sandglass in the other. You can also see a turbaned Turk, a miser, and a vain man admiring himself in a mirror. The complicated clockface shows everything from hours and days to equinoxes and phases of the moon.

According to legend, after the astronomer Master Hanuš put the finishing touches to the clock in 1490, the municipality had him blinded so that he would not repeat his achievement elsewhere. Infuriated by this injustice, Hanuš groped his way up the clock tower and ruined the clock mechanism, which refused to function for 80 years.

Open: Apr–Oct, Mon 11am–6pm, Tue–Sun 9am–6pm; Nov–Mar, Mon 11am–5pm, Tue–Sun 9am–5pm. Guided tours of the interior every hour, and access up the tower (great view). Admission charge.

Kostel Svatého Mikuláše (Church of St Nicholas)

At the northwest corner of the square stands Kilián Ignác Dientzenhofer's marvellously proportioned Baroque church, built for the Benedictines between 1732 and 1735. The interior is less sumptuous than one might expect, perhaps because much was removed when Joseph II turned it into a warehouse in the late 18th century. Since 1920, it has belonged to the refounded Czech Hussite Church.

Open: 10am–noon, 2–5pm, & evenings during concerts. Closed: Mon & Sat.

Staroměstské náměstí is in a pedestrian zone. It is approached by trams 17 and 18, and the metro to Staroměstská, followed by a short walk along Kaprová.

The Baroque Church of St Nicholas presides over the entire district

Palác Kinský
(Kinský Palace)

On the east side of the square is the Kinský Palace of 1765. Franz Kafka attended a school in the palace, and his father kept a haberdashery shop on the ground floor. It houses part of the National Gallery collection, and is the gallery's information centre (including a book and gift shop).
Staroměstské náměstí 12. Tel: (02) 2481 0758. Open: Tue–Sun 10am–6pm.

Kostel Panny Marie Před Týnem
(The Church of Our Lady before Týn)

South of the Kinský Palace is the Venetian-style old parish school (Týnská Škola). Through the third arch from the left access is gained to the Týn Church, built by Petr Parléř's workshop in the 14th century. It was once the stronghold of the moderate Hussites known as Utraquists (*see p122*). Their symbol, a huge gilded chalice, hung on the façade until replaced by a Counter-Reformation image of the Virgin Mary (embellished with gold from the chalice).

The bleak interior contains as highlights Baroque paintings over the high altar by Karel Škréta, a medieval *pietà* in the side-chapel at the east end, and the tomb of Tycho Brahe, on the fourth pier to the right.
Under reconstruction.

U Kamenného Zvonu
(The House of the Stone Bell)

The existence of this remarkable Gothic house (originally Romanesque) was unknown until the 1960s, when a survey revealed the medieval treasure encased

The House at the Golden Unicorn

in a Baroque shell. It is thought to have been a palace for Queen Elizabeth, wife of John of Luxembourg.
Staroměstské náměstí 16. Tel: (02) 2481 0036. Open: 10am–6pm & sometimes for evening concerts on the upper floor.

Dům U Minuty
(House of the Minute)

The most striking aspect of this house, rebuilt in the 17th century in the style of the Lombardy Renaissance, is that its walls are completely covered with mythological and biblical sgraffiti.
Staroměstské náměstí 2. Not open to the public.

U Zlatého Jednorožce
(The House at the Golden Unicorn)

This building reveals several layers of architecture – Romanesque, Gothic, Renaissance, and finally, a Baroque

façade. Bedřich Smetana founded a music school here in 1848.
Staroměstské náměstí 20.
Not open to the public.

U Modré Hvězdy
(House at the Blue Star)
This historic inn has a Romanesque hall below ground, while the brick arcades are Gothic. The *vinárna* (wine bar) here, known as U Bindrů, has been in continuous operation since the 16th century, although it's currently a bit of a tourist trap. Local characters live on in the names of its main dishes which bear such names as 'Hanuš' (of astronomical clock fame), and 'Mydlář' (the executioner of the Protestant nobles in 1621, much admired for his cool way with an axe).

Staroměstské náměstí 25. Tel. (02) 2422 7541. Open: daily 11am–midnight.

Pomník Jana Husa
(The Jan Hus Monument)
On 6 July 1915, the 500th anniversary of the judicial murder of Jan Hus, this vast Art Nouveau monument was unveiled. Ladislav Šaloun's sculpture exudes pathos and patriotism. Hus stands grimly, flanked by 'the defeated' and 'the defiant'. The inscription runs: 'Truth will prevail' – a quotation from Hus's preaching. The monument became a rallying point and emblem of Czech patriotic feeling. For that reason, the Nazis covered it with swastikas in 1939; in 1968, it was draped in black cloth, a sign of mourning for Czech independence crushed by the Soviets.

The Kinský Palace, designed by Kilián Ignác Dientzenhofer

Walk: The Heart of the Old Town

This walk through Prague's historic Staré Město (Old Town) offers a kaleidoscopic tour of the Czech core of the city. *(Follow orange numbers on map for route; for green numbers see* Walk *pp78–9.)*

Allow about 1½ hours.

The point of departure is Staroměstské náměstí (Old Town Square), which is reached on foot from the Staroměstská Metro station (line A) or tram stop (Nos 17 & 18).

1 Old Town Square

In the summer months, Old Town Square *(see pp124–7)* is an ongoing spectacle where you can encounter anything from living sculpture to Hare Krishna devotees chanting and handing out sweets. There are reminders of a Hussite past in the great Kostel Panny Marie Před Týnem (Týn Church) at the east end, and the modern monument to Jan Hus dominating the northern half of the square.

Nearby, Protestant nobles were executed after rebelling against the Habsburgs. In the more recent past, the 1948 Communist takeover was announced by Klement Gottwald to cheering crowds from a balcony of the Palác Goltz-Kinských (Kinský Palace) on the east side. A later generation threw Molotov cocktails as Soviet tanks advanced into the square in 1968.
Leave the square by Železná St and turn right into Havelská.

2 Havelska

On your left is Kostel svatého Havla (St Gall's Church), where early campaigners preached against the abuses of the Catholic hierarchy. Outside, a lively market sells everything from fruit and flowers, to wooden toys and leather goods.
Turn left out of Havelská across Uhelný trh, then left into Rytířská.

3 Rytířská

Halfway down the street is the graceful Stavovské divadlo (Estates Theatre), which Miloš Forman chose for scenes for the film *Amadeus,* since it remains exactly as it was on *Don Giovanni's* first night. As you walk down Ovocný trh beyond the theatre, you will see an ornate Gothic window protruding from the wall of the Karolinum (Charles University, *see p82*). The street ends in Celetná; on the Cubist corner building (No. 34) note the petite *Black Madonna,* a survivor from an earlier Baroque building here.

4 Obecní Dům

A right turn into Celetná brings you under the medieval Prašná Brána

(Powder Tower), and then left, into náměstí Republiky, which is dominated by the Art Nouveau Obecní dům (Municipal House, *see pp120–21*). The independence of Czechoslovakia was proclaimed here in 1918. If you feel like a pause, it contains a spectacularly beautiful café with rather tasty cakes.

Turn left up U Obecního domu, right up Rybná, and left up Jakubská, passing along the side of Kostel Svatého Jakuba (St James's Church), whose entrance is in Malá Štupartská.

5 Kostel Svatého Jakuba

One of the loveliest of Prague's Baroque churches *(see p39)*, St James's is beloved by the locals for its sung masses on Sundays, not least because of its superb acoustics. It has stunning frescoes and an exuberant stucco façade.

At the northern end of Malá Štupartská turn left into Masná, cross Dlouhá and enter Kozí, bearing right into Haštalská, and then turn left into Anežská.

6 Anežská

At the end of the street the Anežský Klášter (St Agnes' Convent, *see pp28–9*) is entered through a gate in the wall. Its fine Gothic architecture and picture gallery, as well as the pleasant summer garden with a café, are worth a visit.

From St Agnes' Convent head for Na Františku, via U Milosrdných and Kozí. It is then a short walk westwards along Na Františku to Pařížká, and the trams at Právnická Fakulta.

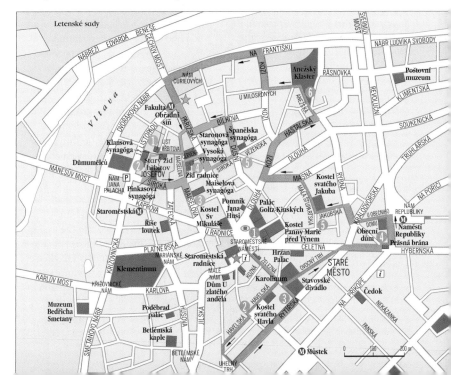

Strahovský Klášter
(Strahov Monastery)

Strahov owes its name to its commanding position on Charles IV's city fortification (*strahovní* means 'to watch over'). The monastery (*see p71*) is approached either from Pohorelec No. 8, up some narrow steps, or through a Baroque archway further east. The arch is crowned with JA Quittainer's statue of St Norbert, founder of the Premonstratensian Order that occupied the monastery after its foundation by Prince Vladislav II in 1140. In 1627, the monks acquired the remains of the saint.

In the courtyard you will pass the deconsecrated **Kostel Svatého Rocha** (Church of St Rock), erected by Rudolf II in gratitude to the saint for his efforts in ensuring that Prague was spared the 1599 plague epidemic. Beyond is the **Kostel Nanebevzetí Panny Marie** (Church of the Assumption). Quittainer's impressive *Immaculata* over the portal provides a foretaste of the rich Baroque interior. Mozart twice played on the church's mighty organ, which has 4,000 pipes and 63 stops.

Close by is a ticket office for visits to Strahov's most spectacular sights, the Teologický sál (Theological Hall) and the Filosofický sál (Philosophical Hall), both libraries. The Theological Hall was built in 1671 with a pleasing barrelled vault by Giovanni Orsi. One of the monks, Siard Nosecký, painted frescoes illustrating man's struggle to acquire wisdom. A similar theme forms the leitmotif of the neighbouring Philosophical Hall, where the ceiling was painted by the great Viennese-trained master, Franz Anton Maulpertsch in 1784. His *Struggle of Mankind to Know Real Wisdom* boldly includes pre-Christian figures, such as Alexander the Great, Aristotle, Plato, Socrates, and Diogenes the Cynic (sitting in his barrel).

Pohořelec 8, Hradčany. Tel: (02) 2451 0355. Open: daily 9am–noon, 1–5pm. Tram: 22 or 23 to Památník písemnictví. Strahov also houses the Památník Národního Písemnictví (National Literature Museum).

Trojský Zámek (Troja Palace)

The red and white painted Troja Palace in Prague 7 is a splendid architectural homage to victory, commissioned by Habsburg loyalist Count Wenceslas Šternberk just after the spectacular defeat of the Turkish armies at the gates of Vienna in 1683. Jean-Baptiste Mathey designed the summer palace with a formal French garden. The grand steps on the garden side are embellished with statues representing the battle between Gods and Titans. In the Great Hall, busts of Habsburg emperors line the wall in the Roman manner, and a huge mural by Dutch artist Abraham Godin shows the triumphal procession of

Baroque ornamentation on the Troja Palace

Theological Hall in the Strahov Monastery, with its magnificent ceiling frescoes

Leopold I after the Turks had been put to flight.

The palace is now administered by the Museum of the City of Prague, and contains a good display of Czech 19th-century painting.

Prague 7 U trojského zámku 4, Troja. Tel: (02) 689 0761. Open: Apr–Oct, Tue–Sun 10am–6pm; Nov, Sat–Sun 10am–5pm. Gardens open: Tue–Sun 10am–5pm all year. Admission charge for palace. Every first Tue in the month is free. Metro: to Nádraží Holešovické, then bus 112.

Stavovské Divadlo (Estates Theatre)

This delightful Neo-Classical theatre was named after the Czech dramatist, Josef Týl, but is usually known as the Stavovské divadlo (Estates Theatre), as it belonged to the Bohemian Diet in the early 19th century. Mozart's *Don Giovanni* and *La Clemenza di Tito* were premiered here.

Ovocný trh 1. Tel: (02) 2421 4339. Performances usually begin at 7pm.

Týnský Dvůr Ungelt (Týn Court or Ungelt)

Týn Court is also known as Ungelt because money (*geld*) was exchanged and customs dues paid here from medieval times up to 1773. The word *týn* (an enclosed area or courtyard) gave the whole complex of architecturally important buildings its name. The site was extended to the neighbouring church and school (*see p126*). Exquisitely renovated, it houses some very up-market cafés, shops, boutiques, and offices.

Immediately northeast of Staroměstské náměstí. Metro: to Můstek.

Václavské Náměstí
(Wenceslas Square)

More of a boulevard than a square, this is the best known part of Prague, although not the most attractive. The area was once a horse market but has long been the focus for political demonstration. The most dramatic events of the Velvet Revolution took place here, including the historic moment when Václav Havel and Alexander Dubček addressed the crowd from the balcony of the offices of the Socialist Party newspaper (No. 36).

The highest end of the square is dominated by the **National Museum**; below that is Josef Myslbek's monumental equestrian statue of St Wenceslas with the four patron saints of Bohemia (1912), a constant rallying point for protest or jubilation. It was here that the student Jan Palach set fire to himself on 16 January 1969. In front of the monument is a small shrine to the victims of Communist repression.

The Buildings

The square is a showcase for 19th- and 20th-century public buildings. There are fine Art Nouveau edifices (the Peterkův dům and the Evropa Hotel – *see p30*), imposing Neo-Renaissance blocks, and some of Prague's better modern architecture, such as the Bata shoe store (Dům obuvy, No. 6). The Hotel Juliš at No. 22 was designed by Pavel Janák and (like the shoe store) is a so-called Constructivist work from the 1920s. Also worth a glance is the leisure complex of the Lucerna Palace (No. 61), built by Václav Havel's grandfather and containing a shabby but beautiful cinema with a horseshoe-shaped piano bar. The Wiehl House at No. 34 is a colourful example of Bohemian Neo-Renaissance.

The area encompassing Václavské náměstí, Národní and Na příkopě is the commercial centre of Prague and known as the Golden Cross. Approach is by metro to Muzeum or Můstek.

Wenceslas Square lit up at night

The Prague section of the Vltava is spanned by 15 bridges (*mosty*). The oldest, **Karlův most** (Charles Bridge (see *pp84–5*) was also the only one up until 1836.

The great era for bridge-building was the late 19th and early 20th century, when the Palacký, Mánes, Čech, and Hlávka bridges were constructed. The **Hlávkův most** was named after a rich contractor who financed its construction. Notable are its two allegorical sculptures of *Humanity* and *Work* by Jan Štursa. The **Čechův most**, named after the romantic poet Svatopluk Čech, has attractive early 20th-century decoration and lamp posts. The historian František Palacký, the father of the Czech national revival, is honoured in the name of the **Palackého most**, a bridge crossed by Albert Einstein twice daily as he walked to and from the university.

The **Most Legií** was inaugurated by Emperor Franz Joseph in 1901, but its name commemorates the Czech legions who fought against his crumbling empire in World War I.

An elaborate lampstand base on the Legií (Legion) Bridge

The **Mánesův most** takes its name from the patriotic painter Josef Mánes, and there is a monument to him standing at the Josefov end.

Bridges seem to be regarded as political barometers, and change their names accordingly. The Mánes Bridge was originally dedicated to the Austrian heir to the throne, Archduke Franz Ferdinand, and the Bridge of the Legions became the Bridge of the First of May under the Communists. Poignantly, the unofficial name for the **Bránický most** is the 'Bridge of the Intelligentsia', because intellectuals were used as forced labour to build it for the Stalinist regime of the 1950s.

Bránický most Trams: 3, 17, & 21.
Palackého most Metro to Karlovo náměstí.
Most Legií Trams, 6, 9, 12, 18, 22, & 23.
Mánesův most Trams 12, 17, 18, 22, & 23.
Čechův most Trams 17 & 12.
Hlávkův most Trams 1, 3, 8, 24, & 25; metro to Vltavská.

Walk: Vyšehrad

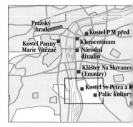

This walk takes you through the ancient citadel of Vyšehrad on its great rock, and offers Prague's finest views of the Vltava.

Allow 2 hours.

Take the metro (line C) to Vyšehrad. Walk west along the terrace of the ugly modern Prague Conference Centre (or KCP), then enter Na Bučance.

1 Táborská Brána

The Tabor Gate of Vyšehrad (meaning 'High Castle') is at the end of the road. Legend says that the Slavic tribes originally settled on this windy outcrop when they reached the Vltava. It was here that Libuše, daughter of an early chieftain, is supposed to have had a vision prophesying the foundation of Prague. She is also said to have had numerous discarded lovers hurled from the top of the cliff into the Vltava. However, the archaeological evidence suggests that Hradčany was settled before Vyšehrad.

Continue along V pevnosti.

2 Leopoldová Brána

Beyond the Leopoldová brána (Leopold Gate), on the right, is the earliest and best preserved of Prague's Romanesque rotundas (Rotunda Svatého Martina/St Martin's). It probably served as a cemetery chapel and was built some time in the 11th century.

Bear left into K rotundě and then right down to the east gate of the Vyšehradský hřbitov (Vyšehrad Cemetery – see p36;

opening times vary, but are usually between 8am & 6pm).

3 Vyšehradský Hřbitov

Leading intellectual figures of the Czech national revival in the 19th century – musicians, writers, sculptors, painters, and scientists – are buried here; but soldiers and politicians are excluded. The most impressive part is the Slavín pantheon commemorating leading figures in the arts – a plinth topped by a sarcophagus guarded by a winged genius.

4 Kostel Svatého Petra a Pavela

A walk through the cemetery brings you to the front of the Kostel Svatého Petra a Pavela (Church of St Peter and St Paul), which has undergone alteration in every conceivable style since it was built in the 11th century. A Baroque gate to the south leads into a park, presided over by Josef Myslbeck's gigantic patriotic sculptures, originally made for the Palackého most (Palacký Bridge). Přemysl and Libuše, founders of the Bohemian dynasty, are nearest to you on the left.

5 Western Bastions

From here a circuit of the western bastions can be made, offering marvellous views of the Vltava streaming sluggishly far below. Note the ruins of a watchtower precariously perched on the almost sheer rock, romantically called 'Libuše's Baths'; actually where goods were hauled up from the river in the Middle Ages.

Cut back across the park to St Peter and St Paul and continue down to the Cihelná brána (North Gate) of the citadel. Those who prefer to head for home at this point can do so by following the Přemyslova down towards Na slupi. Otherwise descend towards the town via Vratislava, then turn right into Hostivítova.

6 Nájemný Obytný Dům

At the bottom, on the corner of Hostivítova and Neklanova (No. 30), is Nájemný obytný dům, a celebrated Cubist building designed by Josef Chochol (*see pp46–7*). Other such buildings can be seen at Neklanova 2, and by walking west along Vnislavova to Libušina No. 3. The latter is Chochol's

ambitious Kovařovičova Villa, with a remarkable façade conceived in diamond shapes and curious zig-zag railings round the garden at the rear.

Re-enter Vnislavova and head towards the embankment. Turn right into Rašínovo nábřeží, and a short way along at No. 78 is where Václav Havel lived. The Art Nouveau apartment block had been built and owned by his grandfather, a successful contractor at the turn of the 20th century, and has now been returned to the family. You will also see the Fred and Ginger building, frequently known as the Dancing House, at the corner of the Rašínovo nábřeží, designed by Frank Gehry in the mid-1990s.

Retrace your steps along Vnislavova and Neklanova, turning left into Přemyslova. Cross the busy Vnislavova and pass under a crumbling railway bridge, beyond which is Na slupi. Trams for the centre can be boarded here.

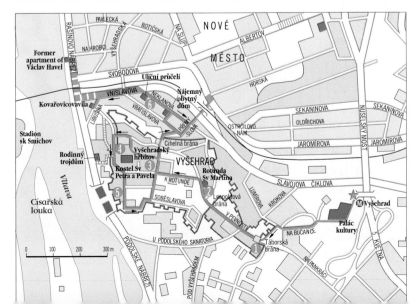

Excursions

Čenský Šternberk
(Bohemian Sternberg)

Southeast of Prague is the impressive stronghold of Čenský Šternberk, built in 1242 on a promontory overlooking the point where the Sázava is joined by its Blanice tributary.

The interior of the castle may be visited as part of a guided tour, and is notable for the Baroque stucco made by Italian craftsmen between 1660 and 1670. Highlights of a visit are the engravings on the staircase of the Thirty Years War, the Yellow Chamber with Carlo Brentano's stucco, and a collection of weapons.

The castle lies 45km southeast of Prague off motorway D1. Tel: (03) 85 5101; Open: Oct–Apr, Sat–Sun & holidays 9am–4pm; May & Sep Tue–Sun 9am–5pm; Jun–Aug, Tue–Sun 9am–6pm.

Hrad Karlštejn (Karlštejn Castle)

The most celebrated Gothic castle of Bohemia was founded by Emperor Charles IV in 1348 and completed by 1357. It was planned as an Imperial and Christian sanctuary. On the highest of its three levels is the Chapel of the Holy Rood, which was also a treasury housing the Crown Jewels of the Holy Roman Empire (now in Vienna) and the Bohemian Regalia. The castle's architect is thought to have been Matthew of Arras, who began the building of St Vitus' Cathedral.

The castle is approached on foot from the railway station. The car and coach

Gothic Karlštejn Castle dominates the surrounding countryside

Regional Map

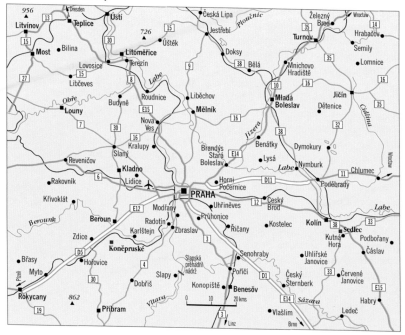

park is 2km below. The interior can only be seen with a guided tour. Highlights include the **Audience Hall**, with handsome wooden panelling and a coffered ceiling, and the **Luxembourg Hall**, which contains a model of how the room looked before the 16th century. The **Church of the Virgin Mary** on the second floor of the north tower is notable for the cycle of frescoes showing the emperor receiving relics from various distinguished donors, and another cycle depicting the Apocalypse. Adjoining the church is **St Catherine's Chapel**, with decoration recalling that of the St Wenceslas Chapel in St Vitus' Cathedral.

The recently restored **Kaple Svatého kříže** (Chapel of the Holy Rood) is the high point of the tour. Its 6-m thick walls are encrusted with 2,200 semi-precious stones, and lined by 128 wooden panels painted by the outstanding court painter, Master Theodoric.

Trains leave for Karlštejn from Smíchovské nádřaži in Prague every hour; the journey takes about 45 minutes. By road it is 28km to the southwest. Tel: (03) 1168 1211. Castle open: Jan–Mar 9am–4pm; May, Jun, & Sep 9am–5pm; Jul–Aug 9am–noon, 12.30–7pm. Admission charge (much higher for foreigners).

Note: if a state holiday falls on Monday, the normal closing day, the castles generally remain open and close on Tuesday instead.

Zámek Konopiště (Konopiště Castle)

This magnificent but gloomy Gothic and Renaissance hunting castle was acquired in 1887 by Archduke Franz Ferdinand d'Este, the heir to the imperial throne. In 1907, he employed an English botanist to cross-breed roses at Konopiště to produce a black variety – a commission that provoked Delphic warnings about black roses bringing war and death. It apparently took the botanist until 1914 to cultivate the rose. That same year Franz Ferdinand was assassinated in Sarajevo, leading to World War I.

The car park is 2km below the castle. You enter through the east tower and walk through a Baroque gateway by FM Kaňka with statues by Matthias Braun. The impressive moat is now perambulated by languid peacocks, but in Franz Ferdinand's day it was occupied by bears.

The guided tours include the St George's Museum, some fine furniture, Habsburg memorabilia, and the royal bathroom. The weapons collection is one of the biggest in Europe, with a number of historically important items.

The 90-hectare park is well worth visiting and has an attractive rose garden, a deer park, and a lake. Weather-beaten Baroque statues add to the romantic atmosphere.

Konopiště is 50km south of Prague. Tel: (03) 012 1366. Open: Apr, Sep & Oct, Tue–Fri 9am–3pm, weekends to 4pm; May–Aug, Tue–Fri 9am–4pm, weekends up to 5pm. Admission charge. A train runs to nearby Beněsov (2km) from

Mělník Castle overlooks the River Labe (Elbe)

Praha hlavní nádraží. Alternatively, take a bus from Florenc terminal.

Zámek Křivoklát (Křivoklát Castle)

Ancient Křivoklát is perched on a ledge jutting out of the forests above a tributary of the Berounka River. The castle was first mentioned in records of the year 1110, and became a Přemyslid residence from the reign of Otakar II (1252–78). Much of what is now to be seen is the result of late Gothic reconstruction under the Jagiello king, Vladislav II (*see p60*) in the late 14th century. Rudolf II's English alchemist, Edward Kelley, imprisoned here, may have died leaping from a tower window in an attempt to escape.

The castle tour takes about an hour, and is well worth it for the remarkable Gothic architecture, the paintings and sculptures, the chapel, and the library.
46km west of Prague. Tel: (03)135 5120. Open: Apr–Jun & Sep–Oct, Tue–Sun 9am–noon, 1–3/4pm; Jul–Aug, daily 9am–5pm; Mar, Nov, & Dec, Sat–Sun 9am–noon. Admission charge. Buses run regularly from Praha-Dejvice and take about 1½ hours. Trains run from Smíchovské nádraží to Beroun, where you must change for Rakovník.

Mělník

The wine-producing town of Mělník has a delightful position overlooking the confluence of the Vltava and Labe (Elbe) rivers. The surrounding vineyards were first planted by Charles IV, who brought French wine expertise to the region.

Sights in the town include the Gothic church, the former Lobkowitz Castle, which houses a collection of Baroque

Hunting is the theme of Konopiště Castle

paintings, and a Regional Museum. Ideally, you should time a visit to include a meal, which can be enjoyed on the terraces overlooking the rivers. This may also provide an opportunity to sample the local wine, of which the Tramín is particularly good.
32km north of Prague. Tel: (02) 0662 6853. Lobkowitz Castle, open: Mar–Apr & Sep, Tue–Sun 9am–4pm; May–Aug 8am–noon, 1–5pm. Closed: Oct–Feb. Admission charge. The bus service from Praha-Dejvice and Praha-Florenc takes about one hour.

Church statuary, Kutná Hora

The prosperity of Kutná Hora – evident from its ambitious, though unfinished cathedral, and handsome burghers' houses – lasted until the mid-16th century. Dwindling reserves and flooding put paid to the mining, and the town rapidly fell into decline.

Chrám Svaté Barbory (Cathedral of St Barbara)

This great Gothic cathedral was financed by the miners and dedicated to their patron saint. Building, initiated by Petr Parléř in the late 14th century, was halted by the Hussite wars. At the end of the 15th century, two of the greatest architects of Prague, Matthias Rejsek and Benedikt Ried, produced the marvellous late-Gothic vaulting inside. There are frescoes showing work in the mint (in the Chapel of the Mintmen), and toiling miners (in the ambulatory).
Open: Tue–Sun, summer 9am–6pm; winter 9am–noon, 2–4.30pm. Admission charge.

Mining Museum

A walk down the sculpture-lined Barborská ulice brings you to the Silver Mining Museum. Its display rooms are in the Renaissance house of one John Smíšek, who became rich by exploiting a private (and illegal) mine in the 15th century. It also houses an exhibition on the history of mining, but most visitors head for the medieval mine down the lane behind the building. At the entrance to the 250m of tunnels is a *trejv*, or horse-drawn hoist.
Barborská ulice 28. Open: Apr–Sep, Tue–Sun 8am–noon, 1–5pm; Oct till 4pm. Admission charge.

Kutná Hora (Kuttenberg)

The name of Bohemia's one-time second largest city (now a UNESCO World Heritage site) means 'mining mountain', a reference to the deposits of silver and copper ore on which its prosperity was founded. The mines were vigorously exploited from the late 13th century, bringing a rapid increase in wealth, and attracting miners (chiefly Germans) from outside Bohemia. The royal mint was founded here at the beginning of the 14th century, and King Wenceslas II summoned experts from Florence to advise him on his coinage. They produced the *pražské groše* (Prague Groschen), a silver coin regarded as sound currency all over Central Europe for several centuries.

Vlašský Dvůr (The Italian Court)

Wenceslas II's mint – known as the Italian Court, after the king's Florentine advisers – later became a royal residence. The bricked-up outlines of the mintmen's workshops can still be seen, together with the chapel and parts of the former palace. Across the square to the west is the Gothic Chrám Svatého Jakuba (Cathedral of St James), built in 1420 with a Baroque interior.
Havlíčkovo náměstí. Open: daily, summer 9am–6pm; winter 10am–4pm. Admission charge.

Other sights worth a visit include Matthias Rejsek's magnificent Stone Fountain (1495) in Husova ulice, and the Kamenný dům (Stone House) off Hornická ulice, with its richly decorated front. The latter is a Gothic burgher's house whose rooms can be visited.

Sedlec

Three kilometres to the north of Kutná Hora is Sedlec, where the star attraction is the Cistercian *kostnice* (ossuary). In the 19th century, František Rint used its approximately 40,000 bones to create what must be one of Europe's most macabre spectacles – an interior decorated with a 'chandelier', 'bells', 'urns', even a Schwarzenberg 'coat of arms', all made from human bones.
*Ossuary open: daily, summer 8am–noon, 1–6pm; winter 9am–noon, 1–4pm.
Buses: 1 & 4 from Kutná Hora to Sedlec.*

Kutná Hora is 68km east of Prague. Many buses run from the Želivského or Florenc terminals in Prague and take about 1–1½ hours. Trains run infrequently from Masarykovo or Hlavní nádraží, but the town's main station is a long way from the sights.

The Cathedral of St Barbara, the patron saint of miners

Lidice

The village of Lidice was razed to the ground by the Nazis on 10 June 1942 in revenge for the assassination of the Bohemian governor, Richard Heydrich, by the Czech resistance. In the village there is a small Memorial Museum, and a Rose Garden of Friendship and Peace planted in 1955.

22km northwest of Prague.
Museum open: daily 8am–4pm.
Regular bus service from Praha-Dejvice.

Terezín

Northwest of Prague in former Sudetenland, Joseph II built a fortified 'town' – in reality, a huge barracks and prison – in 1780, and named it 'Theresienstadt' after his mother, Maria Theresa. In June 1942, the inhabitants were driven out by the Nazis, and the main part of it was turned into a ghetto for Jews.

The Nazis used Terezín for propaganda, allowing the doomed Jews to pursue cultural activities such as music and drama, and building gleaming facilities to show visitors from the Red Cross. The Ghetto Museum has an informative (and harrowing) display, including clips from the propaganda film *Hitler Gives the Jews a Town*.

On the other side of the river that divides the town, the Malá Pevnost (Lesser Fortress) may also be visited. A prison under the Habsburgs (Gavrilo Princip, the murderer of Archduke Franz Ferdinand at Sarajevo in 1914, languished here), it was later used as a concentration camp and extermination centre. There is an exhibition in the former house of the camp commandant. A short documentary film is screened, and you can tour the cells.

60km northwest of Prague. Ghetto Museum open: daily 9am–6pm (4.30pm in winter). Closed: 24–26 Dec & 1 Jan. The Malá Pevnost: Tel: (04) 1678 2255. Open: daily 9am–5pm. Terezín is 1½ hours by bus from Florenc bus terminal. Weekly tours also leave from Josefov (inquire at the ticket office of the State Jewish Museum) and are also run by many guided tour companies in Prague.

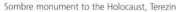

Sombre monument to the Holocaust, Terezín

A commanding presence in a great city: the tower of the Old Town Hall

Getting Away From It All

Boat Trips on the Vltava
From April to September, as long as there is enough water, excursions run both north and south on the Vltava. To the north, they go as far as Roztoky (1 hour 20 minutes), and to the south as far as Štěchovice (3 hours) and Slapy Dam (4 hours). Shorter trips offer a 'panorama of Prague' (50 minutes to 2 hours), and a paddle steamer also operates occasionally. Check details with the Prague Information Service (*www.pis.cz*).

A favourite destination for Praguers who want to get away from it all is **Slapská Přehradní Nádrž** (Slapy Dam), reached via a picturesque 33km stretch of the Vltava Valley. The

Excursion boats are run by Pražská Paroplavební Společnost, (PPS), and leave from the mooring at Palackého most (*tel: 2491 7640*). The nearest metro station is Karlovo náměstí. Lines run to Slapy, Štechovice, Stromovka (and the Zoo). There are organised sightseeing cruises as well as boats for hire.

Monument to the Battle of the White Mountain

65-m high dam was built in 1954, and has 40km of reservoir stretching behind it which is a paradise for watersports and fishing.

Bílá Hora (White Mountain)

On the western outskirts of Prague is White Mountain, where the most decisive battle of Bohemian history was fought on 8 November 1620. On this limestone plateau, the Protestant mercenaries of Bohemia, under Count Thun, were decisively defeated by an imperial Catholic army under Maximilian of Bavaria. The elected Bohemian king (Frederick of the Palatinate) fled, opening the way to three centuries of Habsburg rule. Czechs see this date as marking the end of their independence (not regained until 1918), and the beginning of *temno* (darkness). A small monument marks the site of the battle.

Nearby, to the south, is the **Chrám Panny Marie Vítězné** (Church of St Mary the Victorious), built as a chapel in 1622, and rebuilt as a pilgrimage church between 1704 and 1714. Its interior has fine Baroque frescoes. *The monument is further to the west and along Nad višňovkou; the church is next to the tram stop. Trams: 8 & 22 up to end stop at Řepy. This trip can easily be combined with a visit to the Star Castle (see p83).*

Koněpruské Jeskyně – Český Kras (Koněpruské Caves and the Bohemian Karst)

The Bohemian karst is a protected ecological area, rich in rare flora, but most visitors go to see the stalactite and stalagmite limestone caves. Since their discovery in 1950, 800m of labyrinthine chambers have been made accessible to the public.

Another exciting discovery was the remains of an illegal mint dating from the second half of the 15th century (there is a small exhibition about it). *50 minutes by train from Praha Hlavní nádraží. Open: Apr–Oct Tue–Sun. The visit could be combined with an excursion to Karlštejn; from Srbsko (one stop beyond Karlštejn on the railway), a yellow-marked path leads to the caves (about 3km). A bus connects them with the station at Beroun.*

Kunratickýles (Kunratice Woods)

This extensive area of pleasant woodland southeast of the city is criss-crossed with asphalted paths. A moufflon herd is said to run wild here; there is a mini-zoo at the forester's hut with a few wild boar, deer, and pheasants.

You can walk to the ruin of Nový hrad, known as the 'Stone of Wenceslas' because Wenceslas IV built it as a hunting lodge. Supposedly, it was here, in 1419, that the king had a fatal stroke on hearing of the defenestration of Catholic councillors. There is a restaurant named after the choleric king, U krále Václava IV.

On the west side of the woodland flows the Kunratice River. Several of its pools make informal bathing beaches, mostly around Šeberák. Near here the first nude beach was instituted when such things were still considered extremely daring. *Metro: (line C) to Roztyly.*

Průhonice

Most visitors to the town of Průhonice, on the southeast periphery of Prague, are drawn by the vast and marvellous landscaped botanical park. It has 700 different plants and shrubs, including alpine species and rhododendrons. (The castle, now a botanical research institute, is closed to visitors.)

A regular ČSAD bus service to Průhonice runs from Chodov metro. By car, turn off the D1 motorway, about 10km after leaving the city.

Stromovka Výstaviště

The Holešovice district of Prague has an extensive exhibition area (Výstaviště) for which remarkable buildings were designed in 1891 (*see pp30–31*). Apart from the regular fairs and exhibitions held here, the place is known for its funfair (*Dětský svět*), its **Planetarium**, and the **Maroldovo panoráma**, a diorama of the Battle of Lipany (1434).

The leafy Stromovka Park, stretching to the west of Výstaviště, was planted on the orders of Rudolf II in 1593, and has an artificial lake. You can cross the park and river, and reach both Troja castle and the zoo from here (allow 45 minutes at least).

Signposts for walkers in the woods

Výstaviště open: daily 2pm, weekends 10am. Planetarium: generally open 8am–6pm, but hours vary. Tel: 37 17 46. Maroldovo panoráma open: daily 9am–5pm. Metro: (line C) to nádraží Holešovice. Trams: 5, 12, & 17 to Výstaviště.

Vltava Islands

Ten islands remain from roughly twice that number before the regulation of the Vltava in the late 19th century. The most picturesque is **Kampa**, an island only by virtue of the millstream that separates it from the Malá Strana bank.

Opposite Vyšehrad are **Císařská Louka** (the Emperor's Meadow) on the Smíchov side (a venue for watersports) and **Veslařský Ostrov** off the Vyšehrad/Podoli shore (the haunt of sailors and skullers). **Slovanský Ostrov** (between Jiráskův most and most Legií) has three stations for hiring out rowing boats in summer. All the islands are accessible on foot.

Relaxing in Stromovka Park

Worth a visit – the landscaped garden at Průhonice

Shopping

Prague boasts an ever-growing range of boutiques, shops, and hypermarkets. International brand names in food, furniture, and clothing are certainly in great evidence. Credit cards are widely accepted (EC/MC, and VISA, in particular) in most stores, and you can use almost any card at the many ATMs.

Modern shopping centres – now seen all over

What to Buy

There are a number of items for which Bohemia is famous and which make good souvenirs, particularly glassware. Many antique shops offer attractive Art Nouveau or 19th-century 'historicist' glass items, as well as blue and white 'onion pattern' porcelain. Apart from souvenirs, embroidered textiles are worth considering, as are hand-crafted puppets and wooden toys. Musical mementoes represent good value. Bontonland sells international and local music at prices cheaper than those in the West.

Antiques
Antikvariát 'U Karlova Mostu'
Prints, paintings, rare books, and maps.
Karlova ulice 2, Staré Město.
Tel: (02) 2422 9205.
Antikvariát Karel Křenck
Porcelain, rugs, jewellery, bronzes.
Celetná 31. Tel: (02) 232 2919.

Foreign Language Bookshops
All the following stock books in English:
Big Ben Bookshop
Malá Štupartská 5, Prague 1.
Tel: (02) 231 8021.
Anagram
Týn 4, Prague 1. Tel: (02) 2489 5737.

The Globe
Pštrossova 6, Prague 1.
Tel: (02) 2491 6264.

Department Stores
Kotva
Náměstí Republiky 8, Nové Město.
Tel: (02) 2480 1111. Open until
8pm on Thu.
Tesco
Probably Prague's best food selection is available in the basement of this store.
Národní 26, Nové Město. Tel: (02)
2422 7971. Open: Mon–Fri 7am–8pm,
Sat 8am–8pm, Sun 10am–8pm.
Krone
Václavské náměstí 21, Prague 1.
Open: Mon–Fri 8am–7pm, Sat
8am–6pm, Sun 10am–6pm.
Bilá Labut'
Na Poříčí 23, Prague 1. Open: Mon–Fri
8am–7pm, Sat 8am–6pm, Sun 8am–6pm.

Glass
Along Na příkopě and Celetna are a multitude of shops selling glassware.
Bohemia-Moser
Moser is a top-quality name in Bohemian glass. Mailing service.
Na příkopě 12, Nové Město. Tel: (02)
2421 1293. Also on Malá náměstí 11.

Contrans
Large selection of glass.
Mostecka 11, Malá Strana.

Music
CD Shop – Studio Matouš
Modest but well-chosen selection of
Czech composers.
*Palác Kinských, Staroměstské náměstí.
Tel: (02) 231 1039.*
Bontonland
Václavské náměstí. Tel: (02) 2422 6236.
Popron
*Jurgmannová 30, Prague 1.
Tel: (02) 2494 8682.*

Souvenirs
Blue Praha
Sells glass, gifts, T-shirts, and cards.
*Malá náměstí 14, Prague 1 (and branches
in the centre).*
Botanicus
High-quality, organic, handmade soaps,
oils, candles, and creams.
*Ungelt Týnský dvůr 1049, Prague 1 (and
other centres).*

Czech Traditional Gifts
Handmade toys, traditional fabrics,
metal ornaments, and other reasonably
priced and authentic gift items.
*Melantrichová 17, Prague 1 (and other
branches).*

Clothes
Take a look at *Czech Republic Business
Guide* (*www.neweuropepromotions.cz*)
for comprehensive details of all Prague
clothes stores.

Perfumeries
Lancôme, Christian Dior, Estée Lauder,
and other brand names all have
centrally-based franchises; local
perfumeries include FAnn, Body Basics,
and Occitane (*sold at Country Life,
Melantrichová 14, Prague 1*). Their
branches are dotted all over town.

Prices for many items are now equal to those
of Western Europe. You can now reclaim
VAT on exported items.

Decorated eggs – pretty and inexpensive

Bohemia n Glass

Bohemia means excellent dumplings, beer, and glass. The last two are traditionally inseparable, since the Bohemian glassmakers have probably always needed constant irrigation as they worked at the glass furnaces. Owners were obliged to brew good beer on their estates to keep their glass-making tenants happy, which is doubtless the reason why the quality of both glass and beer has never declined.

The tradition of glassmaking in Bohemia goes back at least to 1414, and possibly as far back as the Celts. The process went on deep in the forests, which supplied the wood for the

furnaces, and glassmakers moved from place to place as wood stocks were exhausted. In the 17th century, the trade separated – makers of raw glass delivered to specialists who cut, engraved, and gilded it. At first, pedlars took the products all over Europe, but by the beginning of the 18th century 'Bohemian Houses' were marketing the famed Czech glass in 38 European ports, as well as America, North Africa, and elsewhere.

During the Renaissance, there were gimmicky innovations (drinking vessels that gurgled or whistled as you drained them); the Baroque period was notable for beautiful engraving on a specially strong glass – Bohemian crystal; the 19th century developed brilliantly coloured glazes. The iridescent Art Nouveau glass of the turn of the 20th century is often even more exotic, with its sensuous shapes and metallic lustre.

Almost all antique shops will have a few pieces of decorative historic glass in the window, while a plethora of crystal

shops will sell you modern crystal of varying quality. The latest fashion is for `old-style' glass made to the designs using traditional techniques in North Bohemia – from Roman to Renaissance to the 1920s. You can spot this glass, thanks to its slightly green tinge. Former US President Bill Clinton has quite a collection.

Bohemian glassware has been produced in Prague since medieval times. Moser is a particularly celebrated brand, though there are galleries exhibiting other unique works by Czech artists and designers of great talent.

Entertainment

There is a lively art scene in Prague, and plenty of galleries. Exhibitions are held in many historic buildings such as the House of the Stone Bell, and the Kinsky Palace on Staroměstské náměstí.

Posters for the State Opera

Art Galleries

Dům U

Top contemporary Czech art is regularly shown in this classic Cubist building.
Černé Matky Boží Ovocný trh 18, Prague 1. Tel: (02) 2421 1732. Open: Tue–Sun 10am–6pm.

Galerie Rudolfinum

Modern, ultra-innovative art.
Alšovo nábřeží 12, Prague 1. Tel: (02) 2489 3205. Open: Tue–Sun, 10am–6pm.

Ivana Follova Art and Fashion Gallery

Offers original glass, ceramics, and clothes to buy and browse through (as well as designer clothes).

Regular art exhibitions are held at the Emmaus Monastery

Ungelt-Tyn 1, Prague 1. Tel: (02) 2489 5460. Open: daily 10.30am–7pm.

Mánes Gallery

The moving spirit behind this gallery was the 19th-century history painter Josef Mánes, who founded an Artists' Association in 1887. The modern building overlooking the Vltava was designed by Otakar Novotný, and incorporates a café.
Masarykovo nábřeží 250, Nové Město. Tel: (02) 29 5577. Open: Tue–Sun 10am–6pm. Closed: Mon.

Theatre

Tickets are available at box offices or through ticket agents: PIS at Na příkopě 20, (*tel: (02) 26 4020*); and at Staroměstské náměstí 1 (*tel: (02) 2448 2018*); and the Mostecká Vez (in summer only), Mostecká 2, Malá Strana (*tel: (02) 536 010*); or Bohemia at Na příkopě 16 (*tel: (02) 2421 5031*); or Malá náměstí 13, Staré Město (*tel: (02) 2422 7832*).

The language barrier will block most visitors' appreciation of Czech theatre, though some contemporary dramatists' works are known through translations, most notably, Bohumil Hrabal and Václav Havel.

The many small or fringe theatres of Prague put on new work, while the **National Theatre**, Národní 2,

Ballet is on offer at the National Theatre (Národní divadlo)

(*tel: (02) 2491 3437*) offers classics as well as ballet and opera. Its Nova Scéna extension stages the multi-media Laterna Magika shows (*see pp102–3*).

'Black' Theatre, Mime, Puppetry

There is now a lot to choose from, and some of the shows are devised with the foreign visitor in mind. The mime tradition of Prague is very sophisticated, and the best shows are memorable.

Divadlo Na Zábradlí
Mime shows as well as straight theatre. *Anenské náměstí 5, Staré Město. Tel: (02) 2222 2026.*

Divadlo Spejbla a Hurvínka
Josef Škupa's famous puppet duo. *Dejvickà 38, Praha-Dejvice. Tel: (02) 32 3351.*

Divadlo Image
Mime and pantomime. *Pařižská 4, Staré Město. Tel: (02) 232 9191, www.imagetheatre.cz.*

Cinema

The tabloid section of the weekly English-language newspaper *Prague Post* (*www.praguepost.cz*) lists films shown in English (foreign films are otherwise dubbed in Czech – indicated on the poster by a small square). The British Council (*Národní 10, Nové Můsto, tel: (02) 2491 2179*) shows English films, and Studio MAT (*on Karovo nam*) shows Czech films with English subtitles from time to time.

Czech cinema is noted for its off-beat humour and deadpan satire. Miloš Forman's early films were examples of this, while the most enchanting of the Czech New Wave films was Jiří Menzel's *Closely Observed Trains* (1966).

For the permanent collections of the **National Gallery**, *see pp108–9*.
Contemporary Czech art is displayed in the **Museum of Modern and Contemporary Czech Art**, Veletržní Palace, Holešovice.

MUSIC

Prague is one of the great centres of music-making in Europe (*see pp106–7*). Since 1989, the opportunities for Czech composers and musicians have broadened considerably and excitingly.

Bohemian musical tradition is rich in Baroque composers and the 19th-century Romantics. For example, a group called Musica Antiqua Praha specialises in Baroque works played on original instruments. Their repertoire includes items of music from the archives of a 17th-century bishop of Olomouc in Moravia, discovered by their director, Paul Kliner. The first privately funded ensemble, the Virtuosi di Praga, concentrates on the music of Mozart. If you want to know more about Czech composers, or would like to buy Czech sheet music, try TALACKO, Rybná 29, Staré Město (English and Czech-speaking). Music can be heard live at the following venues:

Concert Halls
Rudolfinum
Alšovo Nábř 12, Staré Město. Tel: (02) 2489 3352.

Smetanova Síň Obecního domu (Smetana Hall of the Municipal House)
Náměstí Republiky 5, Nové Město. Tel: (02) 2200 2211.
The Bertramka (*Mozartova 169, Smíchov, tel: (02) 54 3893*) and **Vila Amerika** (*Ke Karlovu 20, tel: (02) 29 8214*) hold regular evening performances of Mozart and Dvořák arias (*see pp106–7*). Concerts and recitals take place in many of the city's palaces and churches throughout the year.

Opera
Národní divadlo (National Theatre)
Opera and theatre performances.
Národní 2, Nové Město. Tel: (02) 2490 1448.
Státní opera (State Opera)
Opera and ballet.
Wilsonova 4, Nové Město. Tel: (02) 26 5353.
Stavovske divadlo (Estates Theatre)
Opera, ballet, theatre.
Wilsonova 4, Nové Město. Tel: (02) 2421 5001.

Operetta and Musicals
Hudební divadlo v Karlíně (Karlin Music Theatre)
Křižíkova 10, Karlín, Prague 8. Tel: (02) 2186 8149.

PRAGUE FESTIVALS

The Pražské Jaro (Prague Spring) traditionally begins on 12 May with a performance of Smetana's *Má Vlast* (*My Country*), and closes on 2 June with Beethoven's *9th Symphony*. In between is a rich programme of opera, choral works, chamber music, and recitals given by international stars. In July and August, the Prague Cultural Summer features music, dance, and theatre. Praga Europa Musica in September presents a programme combining aspects of Czech music with music of another European country.

Folk Music

Look for *folklórní skupina* in the listings, or *tel: (02) 2410 2218* for information. *Folklórní Sdruzěni ČR, Senovážné náměsti 24, Nové Město.*

Jazz

Agherta Jazz Centrum

Probably one of Prague's best. *Krakovská 5, Nové Město. Tel: (02) 2221 1275. Open: daily 5pm–1am.*

u staré paní

Dinner, drinks, and good jazz. Reservations essential. *Michalská 9, Staré Město. Tel: (02) 2422 890. Open: daily 6.30pm–4am.*

Metropolitan Jazz Club

Swing, ragtime, blues. *Jungmannova 14, Nové Město. Tel: (02) 2494 7777. Open: Sun–Fri 7pm–1am.*

Reduta Jazz Club

A great survivor. Dixieland, swing, and modern jazz on offer. *Národní 20, Nové Město. Tel: (02) 2491 2246. Open: daily 9pm–midnight.*

Folk dancing in the best Czech tradition

NIGHTLIFE

The ingredients of Prague nightlife are much the same as elsewhere: jazz venues, bars, floor shows, and casinos for the middle-aged or older, clubs, discos, and noisy live-music venues for the young. To get the latest information on the club scene, grab a copy of Czech-English (free) *Think*, available at most English-language video stores, Radost FX Club, and central 'trendy' restaurants. Otherwise, consult ticket agencies, the *Prague Post* (*www.praguepost.cz*), or buy a copy of *Přehled*, a monthly guide to what's on, in Czech, or *Welcome to Prague*, a useful monthly listings guide in a multitude of languages. Note that Wenceslas Square and Betlemské náměstí have a reputation for prostitution, and you should watch your valuables at night in these areas. Lastly, the expensive hotel nightclubs and some more modest places insist on 'correct' dress – no jeans, no trainers, tie obligatory.

Cabaret, Floor Shows

Traditional floor shows are held mainly in hotels. Be sure to reserve your table in advance.

Alhambra (Ambassador Hotel)
Václavske náměstí 5, Nové Město. Tel: (02) 2419 3681.

Esplanade
Washingtonova 19, Nové Město. Tel: (02) 2421 1715/ 2421 3697.

Casinos

There are casinos in **Hotel Corinthia** *Open: 8pm–4am* and the **Ambassador:** *Open: 24 hours.*
Others are:

Casino Atrium
Hilton Hotel, Pobřežní 1, Prague 8. Tel: (02) 2484 1111. Open: daily 2pm–5am.

Casino Royal
Admiral Yacht Club, U Plovárny 8, Prague 1. Open: daily 1pm–6am.

Casino Palais Savarin
Na příkopě 10, Nové Město. Tel: (02) 2422 1636. Open: daily 1pm–3am.

Dancing

Radost FX
Veggie café, superb disco, art gallery, and CD shop.
Bělehradská 120, Prague 2. Tel: (02) 2425 4776; www.radostfx.cz

Akropolis
Arty and ethnic events; very laid-back.

BOOKING FOR MUSICAL PERFORMANCES

Tickets for music events can be obtained at the box offices, or from agencies such as **Bohemia** at Na příkopě 16, *tel: (02) 2421 5031, www.ticketsbti.osad.cz.* From mid-April tickets for the Prague Spring Music Festival are on sale at **Hellichova 18** (*www.festival.cz*). Tickets for the Czech Philharmonic are sold at the **Alsovo Kabfieľí** 12, Staré Město, *tel: (02) 2489 3352,* and through **TICKET PRO**, Salvátorská 7. *www.ticketpro.cz*

Kubelíkova 27, Prague 3.
Tel: (02) 2271 2287.

Bílý Koníček

Located in a Romanesque
cellar. Old and new dance
hits. Seedy, but romantic.
Staroměstské náměstí 20.
Tel: (02) 2422 0947.
Open: daily 8pm–5am.

Classic Prague Club

Uses the auditorium of a
theatre for dancing after
performances. Classics of
rock and pop. Friendly
atmosphere.
Pařížská 4, Staré Město.
Tel: (02) 232 0183.
Disco 10.30pm–3am.

Lucerna

Dinner, 'Bohemian
Fantasy' floor show and
dancing. All-in price or
separate booking for
show only.

Štěpánská 61, Nové Město.
Tel: (02) 2421 7108.
Show starts at 9pm.

Lucerna Music Bar

Daily programme starts
at 9pm. New on the
Prague scene.
Vodičkora 36, Nové Město.
Tel: (02) 2421 7108.
Open: daily 7pm–6am.

Klub Lávka

Dancing on a terrace
overlooking the Vltava
with a café and theatre.
Novotného lávka 1, Staré
Město.
Tel: (02) 2421 4797.
Open: 24 hours (dancing
in the evening).

Rock Scene and Gigs

To catch the latest
happenings you must
study the listings in

Prognosis (fortnightly),
Golem (monthly), the
Czech Program (weekly),
or *Přehled* (monthly).

Bunkr

This restaurant was
actually a bunker for
Husák and comrades.
Czech and foreign bands
three weeks in the month,
otherwise disco. Café
upstairs.
Lodecká 4, Staré Město.
Tel: (02) 2317 922.
Open: 8pm–6am.

Rock Café

Hard rock and thrash
metal. Sometimes live
bands. Loud. T-shirts, etc,
on sale.
Národní 20, Nové Město.
Tel: (02) 2491 4416.
Open: daily 10pm–3am
(Sat & Sun 8pm–3am).

Prague nightlife offers many options

Children

Prague is rich in possibilities for keeping children absorbed and contented. There is always plenty going on in Old Town Square (Staroměstské náměstí), and the river is another attraction. Caves, museums, puppets, and a funfair also beckon.

Children enjoying a fiacre ride in the Old Town Square

You could begin with the all-action astronomical clock in Old Town Square and follow up with a tour of the sewers (entrance to the right of the clocktower). In summer, the square is alive with strolling players, ice-cream vendors, and booths selling food and souvenirs. A miniature train leaves from here and runs along Pařížská, over Cechův most and on to Hradčany. Horse-drawn carriages leave from the square for an hour-long tour of the Staré Město.

Another obvious attraction is the river. Cruises start from Palackého most, Rašínovo nábřeží (*for information call (02) 29 3803 and (02) 29 8309*) and go both upstream and downstream. The

longest round-trip lasts more than seven hours, so check timetables and destinations carefully. On a sunny day, fun and exercise may be had by hiring a rowboat from Kampa Island, or the island called Slovanský ostrov or Žofín off Masarykovo nábřeží.

Caves

The stalactite caves of Koněpruské jeskyně in the karst region around Karlštejn offer an exotic alternative excursion. If the children are too small to attempt the 3-km walk from Srbsko station, an infrequent bus runs between Beroun and the caves. Beroun is 50 minutes by train from Praha Hlavní nádraží (*see p145*).

Cinema

The American Hospitality Centre, Malé náměstí 14 (*tel: (02) 2422 5502; open daily 10am–11pm*) is an oasis of American culture (including popcorn and Coca-Cola) much frequented by the young. Films for children are shown here on Saturday mornings.

McDonald's

There are now several in Prague; the central ones are at Vodičkova 15, and on the east side of Wenceslas Square.

Puppets to delight the young and old

Mirror Maze

Petřín Hill is ideal for an excursion with younger children, involving the funicular railway from Újezd, the astronomical observatory, the mini-Eiffel Tower, and the Bludiště (mirror maze), which never fails to appeal and delight.

Museums

The two military museums – in the Schwarzenberg Palace on Hradčany Square (up to World War I – rich collection of early weapons), and in Žižkov (post-1914) – will no doubt fascinate older children. The view from the Czech Army Museum in Žižkov is one of the best in Prague. The huge equestrian monument of the Hussite general Jan Žižka, in front of the museum, is in the *Guinness Book of Records* as the largest sculpture in the world.

The Museum of Flying and Cosmonauts is worth the longish trek, but the National Technical Museum is even more guaranteed to be a hit with the young. The highlights are the automobiles, the motorbikes, the astronomical instruments, and a complete mock-up of a coal mine.

Puppet Theatres
Divadlo Minor

Continuous programmes for children. *Senovážné náměstí 28. Tel: (02) 2421 3241. Metro: to Náměstí Republiky.*
Národní Divadlo Marionet

Matinée performances.
Žatecká 1. Tel: (02) 23 2536. Trams 17 & 18. Metro: to Staroměstská.

Animal magic enthralling young visitors in Prague Zoo

Výstaviště

Funfair, big wheel, planetarium, and other attractions.
Tel: (02) 37 1746 (Planetarium); (02) 201 3204 (Výstaviště). Open: Mon–Fri 2–5pm, Sat–Sun 11am–5pm.

Zoo

An ever-popular location for a day out. *In Troja (7th District). Tel: (02) 6641 0480. Open: daily 9am–7pm, 4pm in winter. Metro: to Nádraží Holešovice, then take bus No. 112.*

The museums mentioned here are covered in detail with full addresses and opening hours on *pp96–101*; only aspects of specific interest to children are stressed here. Likewise, Koněpruské Jeskyně is featured on *p145*, Petřín Hill on *pp118–19*, Výstaviště on *p146*, and cruising on *p144*.

Sport and Leisure

The most passionately followed sports in Prague are football and ice hockey. The latter famously sparked riots in 1969, when the Czech team humiliated the Soviet Union. This was seen as sweet revenge for the Warsaw Pact invasion of the previous year. The Czechs continue to win the World Ice Hockey Championships with almost monotonous regularity.

State-of-the-art pools cater to a popular sport

Billiards

You can play billiards pretty much all over town – look for signs 'Billiard Clubs'.

Bowling
Hotel Corinthia

Just four lanes (but the ten types of beer are a compensation).
Kongressová 1. Tel: (02) 6119 1326. Open 2.30pm–12.30am. Metro: to Vyšehrad.

Bicycles offer easy access to the countryside

Bowling Club

Bowling, billiards, and a bar.
Bořivojovna 83, Prague 3.
Tel: (02) 2272 1549.

Fitness Centres

Aerobic courses, fitness centres, and gyms have mushroomed in Prague recently. Two with good reputations are:
The World Class Health Academy
Top-class, fiendishly expensive gym and pool, with numerous excellent classes (below the Marriott Hotel).
Millennium Plaza, V Celnici 10, Prague 1. Tel: (02) 2421 6896.
YMCA
Pool, gym, and aerobics.
Na Poříčí 12, Prague 1. Tel: (02) 2487 2004. Open: 7am–11pm.

Golf

Czech golfing opportunities are booming, with superb courses in Karlovy Vary, Marianské Lázně (Marienbad), and Karlštejn. They also include the country's best indoor facility and driving range. Call the Czech Golfing Association for further details.
Strakonická 510, Prague 5. Tel: (02) 5732 1229. Open: daily 8am–11pm.

Horse Racing

Steeplechasing and hurdles take place
May to October on Sunday afternoons;
trotting all the year round.
Velká Chuchle. Tel: (02) 54 3091.
Admission fee. Buses: 129, 172, 241, 244,
& 245, from Smíchovské nádraží.

Ice Hockey

Try the Paegas Aréna (*Za Elektrárnou*
419, Prague 7) or HC Slavia Praha
(*Vladivostocká 1460, Prague 10*), and
check local listings for match details at
www.hokej.com

Ice Skating

There are a number of rinks, most with
erratic opening times.
HC Praha
Na rozdíly 1, Prague 6. Tel: (02) 36 2759.
Open: winter only, Sat 3–5pm, Sun
3.30–5.45pm. Metro: to Dejvická, then
tram 26 to Bořislavka.
Zimní Stadión Nikolajka
U Nikolajky 28, Prague 5. Tel: (02) 54
7258. Open: winter only, Sat & Sun
1–4pm. Metro: to Anděl. Trams: 4, 6, 7, 9,
12, 14, & 16.

Football (Soccer)

The leading teams are called Sparta
Praha and Slavia. Check details at:
www.fotbal.cz and *www.czech-fotbal.cz*

Squash

Squash courts are becoming increasingly
legion. The Squash Centrum is in the
heart of Prague, but you can also find
courts at Club Hotel Praha and Hotel
Corinthia.
Squash Centrum: Václavské náměstí 15,
Prague 1. Tel: (02) 2423 2752.

A future Ivan Lendl?

Swimming

Swimming in the River Vltava is not
recommended. There are plenty of
pools, but not all are as clean as they
should be. Those recommended are at:
Plavecký Stadión, Podolská 74, Podolí.
Tel: (02) 4143 3952. Opening hours vary.
Trams: 3, 16, 17, & 21 to Kublov.

Tennis

Czech Tennis Federation.
Štvanice ostrov. Tel: (02) 232 4601.
Open: 6am–dusk. Metro: to Florenc.
Sparta
17 outdoor and two indoor courts.
Stromovka. Tel: (02) 32 4850.
Open: Apr–Oct, 6am–9pm.
Metro: to Hradčanská, then bus 131 to
Nadraží Bubeneč.

Food and Drink

Czech cuisine has traditionally been strong in the meat department (per capita meat consumption under the Husák regime rose to half a kilo per person per day), and correspondingly weak in vegetables. The heavy dishes come from the heartlands of Bohemia, Moravia, and Slovakia. German influence is evident in the various (delicious) sausages and the ubiquitous pickled cabbage. A welcome relief from red meat is provided by the freshwater fish (carp and trout) and increased imports of sea fish. Nevertheless, the typical national dish remains roast pork with cabbage and dumplings. Dumplings are the real glory of Bohemian cuisine. Of course, visitors to Prague can enjoy pizza, vegetarian, ethnic, and international cuisine throughout the capital.

Typical Dishes and Specialities
Soups (Polévka) and Entrées (Předkrmy)
Bramborová polévka: potato soup
Čočková: lentil soup

Fazolová polévka: bean soup
Hovězí vývar: consommé, bouillon
Kulajda: creamy egg and dill soup
Chléb: chewy brown bread

Traditional pork dish

KNEDLÍKY (BOHEMIAN DUMPLINGS)

Dumplings are made from bread, potato dough, soft curd, or flour. Usually served as accompaniments to meat dishes, they also come in more sophisticated guises, the best being fruit dumplings. Here is a recipe for fruit dumplings made from potato dough. *Ingredients: 800g boiled potatoes, 10g salt, 2 eggs, 100g semolina, 200g wholemeal flour, a teaspoonful cinnamon, fresh fruit for filling.*

Peel cold boiled potatoes and grate them. Sprinkle with flour, semolina, and salt. Make a well in the mixture for the eggs. Knead into dough and form pancakes. Add the fruit, close the mixture into balls and seal them. Place in boiling water and cook for 20 minutes. Remove and sprinkle with cinnamon, breadcrumbs fried in butter, or with poppy seeds and sugar. Melted butter or whipped cream make good toppings.

Chlebíčky: open sandwich
Pražská šunka: Prague ham
Pražská šunka s křenem: Prague ham with horseradish
Pražská šunka s okurkou: Prague ham with pickle
Tresčí játra: cod's liver
Uzený jazyk: smoked tongue
Vajíčkový salát: egg in mayonnaise
Omeleta: omelette
Žampióny s vejci: mushroom with eggs
Smažený sýr: hot fried Edam in breadcrumbs

Main Courses
Biftek s vejcem: beef and eggs
Dršťky: tripe
Guláš: goulash
Hovězí: beef
Játra: liver
Kachna: duck
Klobásy: sausages
Knedlíky: dumplings
Krůta: turkey
Kuře: chicken
Skopové: mutton
Smažený řízek: Wiener Schnitzel
Svíčková na smetaně: roast loin of beef with cream sauce
Telecí: veal
Vepřové se zelím: roast pork with sauerkraut

A variety of meats are available and consumed

Vegetables (Zelenika)
Brambory: potatoes
Červená řepa: beetroot
Cibule: onions
Hranolky: French fries
Kyselé zelí: sauerkraut
Lečo: ratatouille
Obloha: garnish (usually pickled vegetables)
Okurka: cucumber
Rajčata: tomatoes
Salát: salad
Špenát: spinach
Zelí: cabbage

Fish (Ryby)
Kapr vařený s máslem: boiled carp with melted butter
Pečená štika: roast pike
Platýs: flounder
Pstruh na másle: trout in melted butter

Dessert (Zákusky)
Jablkový závin: apple strudel
Omeleta se zavařeninou: jam omelette

Palačinky: pancakes
Švestkové knedlíky: plum dumplings (always delicious)
Zmrzlina: ice cream

Cheese (Sýr)
Bryndza: goats' cheese in brine
Oštěpek: smoked curd cheese
Tvaroh: curd cheese
Uzený sýr: smoked cheese
Balkansky sýr: feta cheese

Fruit (Ovoce)
Banán: banana
Borůvky: bilberries
Broskev: peach
Hroznové víno grapes
Hruška: pear
Jablka: apple
Kompot: stewed fruit
Jahody: strawberries
Maliny: raspberries
Pomeranč: orange
Švestky: plums

All ready and waiting to welcome customers at a streetside café

Where to Eat

Although the city's restaurants offer some of the most atmospheric medieval and Baroque interiors in Europe, it cannot be said that the food and services have always lived up to the mark. However, things are now noticeably improving – the variety and standard of eateries is on the up-and-up. Check *www.gurman.cz* for good listings and the latest hotspots, or buy a copy of *Gourmet*. If your meal proves to be in order and if the service has been halfway acceptable, a tip of 10 per cent is usual in top-notch establishments, a few crowns elsewhere. Note that opening times may change slightly, according to season.

Reservations are vital for restaurants, especially in the high season. The most popular places may need to be booked as much as a week in advance, although two to three days is usually adequate. If you have not booked anywhere, you may have to fall back on a beer cellar, a café, or a fast-food outlet.

Types of Eating House

The choice of establishments falls into three main categories: *restaurace* (restaurant), *vinárna* (wine bar or wine cellar), and *pivnice* (beer cellar). The last named usually offers pub food, although that should be regarded in most cases simply as an accompaniment to the serious business of beer consumption. Creeping gentrification has meant that the distinctions between different types of hostelry have become blurred: in particular, a number of *vinárna*s are now luxury restaurants in all but name. Because of inflation and changes of ownership, the following guide to prices can only be an indication. Average meal prices in Koruna Ceska (kč), inclusive of wine, are for a two-course meal for two.

★   up to 500kč
★★   501kč to 1000kč
★★★   1001kč to 1500kč
★★★★ 1501kč to 3000kč

Prices can be expected to continue rising, especially in the sort of place largely frequented by foreigners (already beyond the means of all but a minority of Czechs). The price of a glass of wine varies, but 60kč for a quarter litre is not unusual. Beer prices show even greater disparities – anything from around 12kč in a traditional pub to 60kč or more in a popular tourist spot such as U Flecků.

Czech Cuisine

Klub Architektů ★

A cellar restaurant offering well-cooked staples such as fried cheese, particularly good with apple and cream sauce, and some fine beers.

Betlemské náměstí 5a.
Tel: (02) 2440 1214.
Open: daily
11.30am–midnight.
Metro: to Národni třída.

Restaurace Pivovarský Dům ★

A friendly in-house brewery (the staff may be rushed off their feet, but only because the food and beer are satisfyingly good and demand is huge), creatively decorated with paraphernalia associated with the trade.

Lipova 15, Nové Město, Prague 2.
Tel: (02) 9621 6666.
Open: daily 11am–11pm.
Metro: IP Pavlova.

U Vladáře ★★★

Game and traditional Czech cuisine, served with flair and in huge portions, plus local wines (fair) and beer (unbeatable).

Maltézské náměstí 10 (Malá Strana). Tel: (02) 5753 1309. Open: daily 11.30am–midnight.
Metro: Malostranská.
Trams: 12, 22, & 23.

Knights of Malta ★★★★

Up-market and impressive, and resonating with history. Has become quite a business haunt too.

Prokopská 10, Malá Strana.
Tel: (02) 5753 3666.
Metro: Malostranská.

Some of the national dishes are exceptionally filling, especially with a large mug of beer

French cuisine and Art Nouveau in the Obecní dům

International Cuisine

David ★★★★
Small, exquisite, and chic.
Good salad and poultry.
Tržistě 21. Tel: (02) 53 9325. Open: daily noon–3pm, 6–11pm. Trams: 12, 22, & 23 to Malostranské náměstí.

Nebozízek ★★★
Reached by the funicular railway on Petřín, celebrated as much for the wonderful view as for the game and Bohemian cooking.
Petřínské sady 411. Tel: (02) 53 7905. Open: daily 11am–6pm, 7–11pm. Trams: 6, 9, 12, & 22 to Újezd, then via railway.

Opera-Grill ★★★★
A small establishment offering snails, lobster and salmon – and a pianist!
Karolíny Světlé 35. Tel: (02) 2222 0518. Open: daily 7pm–2am. Metro: to Národní třída. Trams: 6, 9, 18, & 22 to Národní divadlo.

U Zátiší ★★★★
Nouvelle cuisine comes to Prague! Now something of a golden oldie, the fish and duck are highly recommended.
Liliová 1. Tel: (02) 2422 8977. Open: daily noon–2.45pm, 6–10.45pm. Metro: to Národní třída.

Fish Restaurants

Rybí Trh ★★★
Superb fresh fish and seafood and *al fresco* dining in summer.
Týn 4, Staré Město. Tel: (02) 2489 5447. Open: daily 11am–midnight.

Reykjavík ★★★
Fast-frozen Icelandic fish that tastes absolutely fresh: salmon, shrimp, cod, haddock. Fish soup is a speciality. Service excellent; no reservations.
Karlova 20. Tel: (02) 2222 1218. Open: daily 11am–midnight. Metro: to Staroměstská.

Kampa Park ★★★★
Very swanky, elegant restaurant run by a Swede, with one of the best river views in town.
Nakampě 8b, Malá Strana. Tel: (02) 5731 3493. Open: daily 11.30am–midnight.

Radisson Hotel
The superbly renovated old Alcron hotel. Probably Prague's top fish restaurant, under uber-chef Zdcnek Polhreich.
Štěpánská 40, Nové Město. Tel: (02) 2282 0038. Open: Mon–Sat 6pm–10.30pm.

Game Restaurants

Myslivna ★★★
Traditional game restaurant.
Jagellonská 21 (Prague 3). Tel: (02) 627 0209. Open: daily noon–4pm, 6–11.30pm. Metro: to Flora.

U Lípy (At the Lime-Tree) ★★★★
Wide range of game, including hare, quail, and wild boar. Good wine list.
Plzeňská 142. Tel: (02) 52 2927. Open: daily 11am–3pm, 6pm–midnight. Trams: 4 & 9 to Krematorium Motol.

Hájovna (The Gamekeeper's Lodge)
Great venison and other Czech dishes, largely

game as the name implies.
Ondříčková 29, Žizkov, Prague 3.
Tel: (02) 627 0193.
Open: daily 11am–11pm.

Ethnic Restaurants
Chinese
Huang He ★
Off the beaten track, but arguably the best Chinese restaurant in Prague. Hurried, noisy, with delicious grub (booking essential).
Vršovická 1, Vršovice, Prague 10.
Tel: (02) 7174 6651.
Open: daily 11am–11pm.

French
La Provence ★★/★★★
Basement Provençal restaurant (specialities include *lavender crème brulée*) with a raucous bar upstairs and an oyster bar in season.
Štupartská 9, Staré Město.
Tel: (02) 2481 6696.
Open: daily 11am–1am.
Metro: Náměstí Republiky or Můstek.
Vas-y Vas-y ★★
Very relaxing. Great food, good wine.
Pštrossova 8, Nové město.
Tel: (02) 29 1352. Open: daily 11.30am–midnight.
Metro: Karlovo náměstí.
Trams: 6, 9, 22, & 23.

Indian and Pakistani
Jewel of India ★★★
Superb cuisine, an authentic tandoor oven, extensive and innovative menu, a library of Indian cookbooks and guide books.
Pařížská 20, Staré Město.
Tel: (02) 2481 1010.
Metro: Staroměstská.
Mailsi ★/★★
Off-the-beaten-track eatery, friendly service, and faultless Pakistani cuisine.
Lipanská 1, Zizkov, Prague 3. Tel: (02) 9005 9706. Tram: 5.
Taj Mahal ★★
Worth reserving a table. Fiery cuisine, live sitar and other music.
Škrétova 10, Vinohrady, Prague 2.
Tel: (02) 2422 5566.
Metro: Museum.

Thai
Arzenal ★★★
Artistic with fresh and authentic cuisine. Style gallery and shop.
Valentinská 11, Staré Město. Tel: (02) 2481 7479. Open: Wed–Mon 10am–midnight.

Italian
Pizza Coloseum ★
Packed basement pizzeria serving fresh and ample salads, pasta, and classic Italian staples. Good beer too.
Vodičkova 30, Nové Město.
Tel: (02) 2423 3733.
Open: daily 11am– midnight (reservations not possible). Metro: Můstek.

Russian
Ruský Samovar ★★★★
Very pricey, good cooking, and security-conscious. Look out for the stuffed bear by the door.
Dittrichova 25, Nové Město. Tel: (02) 299 011.
Open: daily 6pm–1am.
Metro: Karlovo náměstí.

There is no dearth of places to eat and drink

Refreshment at the sign of the Golden Stag

What to Drink

The two major wine-growing areas of former Czechoslovakia are around Břeclav in Southern Moravia and Pezinok in Western Slovakia. Both regions are near enough to Prague for pleasant weekend excursions; these can be a lot of fun (and pretty alcoholic) during the wine harvest season from mid-September to late October. The picturesque Moravian *sklípeks* (wine cellars) that border the vineyards offer opportunities for wine-tasting, dancing, and eating until you explode. Neither the Czech lands nor Slovakia can truthfully be described as producing classic wines, but the best of them are pleasantly drinkable. The consensus is that Moravian wine outshines the rest,

and many of the Prague cellars specialise in their products. Good wine is also made at Mělník which is near enough to the capital for a lunch or dinner outing (*see p139*).

Wines

The white wine is generally more favoured than the red, and almost invariably drunk within a couple of years of the harvest. *Sauvignon*, which is aromatic with a flavour of ripe peaches, is often an exception to this general rule – the best is said to come from Velké Pavlovice in Moravia. *Ryzlink rýnský*, claimed to be the 'king of wines and the wine of kings', has a bouquet of lime blossom and is good with fish. *Rulandské bílé* is more full-bodied and often likened to a Burgundy. Connoisseurs of Austrian wine will warm to the *Veltlínské zelené*, the fresh, somewhat acidic 'Grüner Veltliner'. Czechs do not mind drinking white wine with roasts, but for this they will probably choose a *Neuburské* (Neuburger) with its slightly smoky taste.

Müller Thurgau is good with fish or veal, while *Silván* is suited to pâté and chicken. A fine Moravian Riesling with limited production is *Bzenecká lipka*, often drunk with grilled meat. Of the reds, *Rulandské červené* has some of the characteristics of a Burgundy, while the velvety *Vavřinecké* wins praise from red wine enthusiasts.

Vinárny and Wine Bars

Prague has a vast number of 'wine cellars' and cocktail and wine bars. Here are some recommendations:

Barock ★★★

Very swanky hangout with cocktails, sushi and glamorous clientele.
Pařížska 24, Staré Město. Tel: (02) 232 9221. Open: daily noon–midnight. Metro: Staroměstská.

Bazaar ★★

Strictly a restaurant, Bazaar is a flamboyant labyrinth of rooms with a wild cabaret and decor, drinks and cocktails.
Nerudova 40, Malá Strana. Tel: (02) 9005 4510. Open: daily noon–midnight. Trams: 12, 22, & 23.

Gargoyle's ★★/★★★

Slick Californian and French cuisine, washed down with a good selection of local and international wines; fine tasting 'gourmet' menu.
Opatovická 5, Staré Město. Tel: (02) 2491 6067. Open: 11am–2pm, 6pm–midnight. Metro: Národní.

Ostroff ★★★

Although not strictly a wine bar, this does have a superb view over the river. The island-based restaurant is high-scale Italian, with correspondingly good wines, and has one of Prague's longest cocktail bars.
Střelecky Ostrov (Sharp-shooters' Island) 336, Staré Město. Tel: (02) 2491 9235. Open: Mon–Fri noon–2pm, 7–11.30pm; Sat 7–11.30pm, Sun 11am–3pm, 7–11.30pm. Metro: Národní třída.

U Sádlů ★

A down-to-earth basement medieval theme pub, with wine, huge beers, and traditional Bohemian and Moravian dishes in an atmosphere of shields, stone, and wooden refectory tables.
Klimentská 2, Staré Město. Tel: (02) 248 13874. Open: daily 11am–1am. Metro: Náměsti Republiky.

A cheerful wine bar sign welcomes you in

Pivnice (Beer Halls)
U Betlémské Kaple ★
Bohumil Hrabal wrote lyrically about the *12° prazdroj* beer served here 'with its marvellous head . . . like whipped cream'. The pub is good value and offers tasty food.
Betlémské náměstí 2.
Tel: (02) 2421 1879.
Open: daily 11am–11pm.
Metro: to Národní třída.
U Dvou Slunců (The Two Suns) ★★
This Baroque house, where the writer Jan Neruda once lived, is now a congenial restaurant serving three sorts of beer from the barrel, and Czech cuisine.
Nerudova 47. Tel: (02) 53 8924. Open: 11am–11pm. Trams: 1 & 22 to Malostranské náměstí.
U Fleků ★★
The sweetish black ale, made since 1843 to a Bavarian recipe, is brewed and sold only on the premises of this five-centuries old brewery. It is best to sit in the garden – brimming mugs arrive automatically, and there are normally one or two hot dishes of the day to choose from.
Křemencova 11. Tel: (02) 2491 5118. Open: daily 9am–11pm. Trams: 3, 9, 14, & 24 to Lazarská.

U Kalicha (The Chalice) ★★
This was *The Good Soldier Švejk*'s favourite watering hole; the place is very touristy, but the food and Pilsner are excellent. Reservations advisable.
Na bojišti 12. Tel: (02) 29 0701. Open: 11am–11pm. Metro: to IP Pavlova.

Kavarna (Cafés)
Jazz Café č.14
Recorded jazz and great coffee makes this an intelligentsia hang-out.
Opatovická 14.
Tel: (02) 2492 0039.
Open: Mon–Fri 10am–11pm, Sat–Sun noon–11pm. Metro: Národní.
Café Evropa
Indifferent menu but superb Art Nouveau interior and nostalgic evening musical duo.
Václavske náměstí 29.
Tel: (02) 2422 8117.
Open: daily 9am–11.30pm. Metro: to Muzeum or Můstek.
Café Savoy
Enjoy the painted Neo-Renaissance ceiling and Viennese interior of this beautifully restored café.
Vitězná 1.
Tel: (02) 53 9796.
Open: daily 9am– 11pm. Trams: 9 & 22 to Újezd.
Café Milena
A reasonably priced Old

CAFÉ CULTURE

Most of the coffee-houses listed are worth visiting if only for the nostalgic atmosphere. They should serve a range of coffees and, minimally, nuts, strudel, and, of course, cigarettes!

In the dozens of ale-houses in Prague you will come across a wide range of beers, food, and prices. Most pubs are tied to the products of one brewery – Pilsner Urquell, Budvar. Often the beers will be from one of the breweries in Prague itself or from the Czech regions.

Town Square café scene with a superb view of the astronomical clock. *Staroměstské náměsti 22. Tel: (02) 26 0843. Open: 10am–10pm.*
Obecní Dům (The Municipal House) Another fine Art Nouveau interior. A pleasant place to write your postcards home, and nosh coffee and cakes. *Náměstí Republiky 5. Open: 7.30am–11pm.*

Metro: to Náměstí Republiky.
Slavia
The famous writers' (and dissidents') Art Deco café, but service is slow. *Národní 1. Tel: (02) 2422 0957. Open: daily 8am–midnight. Trams: 6, 9, 18, 22, & 23 to Národní Divadlo.*

Fast Food/Snacks/ Simple Meals
McDonald's, Kentucky Fried Chicken, Dunkin' Donuts, and Pizza Hut are all here – you can find branches on and near Wenceslas Square.

Vegetarian
Country Life
Takeaway service and cafeteria. *Melantrichova 15, Jurgmannova 1. Tel: (02) 2421 3366. Open: Sun–Fri 8am–7pm. Metro: to Můstek.*

Potato pancakes are irresistible

Beer, to the true-born Czech, is not so much a drink as a way of life. It is nearly impossible to drink an unpalatable brew in Prague, and aficionados of brands are as passionately divided in their enthusiasm as the supporters of the city's two football clubs.

The distinctive, bottom-fermented *Plzeňský prazdroj* (Pilsner Urquell) was first produced in the Bohemian town of Plzeň in 1842. Its great rival is Budvar from *České Budějovice* (Budweis). Flavoured with the hand-picked 'red' hops of Bohemia, the secret of these tipples (as of Scotch whisky) is the soft water used in the brewing. A high carbon dioxide content ensures a fine, flowery head: to test the quality, Praguers stand a matchstick in the foam. The contents are satisfactory if it stays erect for at least ten seconds. Mercifully, Czech breweries have stuck to traditional ingredients and methods, which means the beer-drinker is spared the characterless chemical fizz cynically foisted on Western consumers.

The seriousness of these drinking matters may be seen from the founding of a Party for the Friends of Beer after the Velvet Revolution. Its members appointed themselves guardians of beer quality in the capital, which naturally involved them in the onerous duties of rigorous testing and consumption. Unfortunately, the party has been unable to prevent a scandalous rise in prices, although connoisseurs will whisper to each other the names of a few places that still serve pils at 15kč or less. The discovery that one well-known hostelry had recently raised its prices to an unheard-of 50kč per glass provoked national outrage. A country whose president once worked as a brewery hand does not take kindly to profiteering with a commodity so close to a Czech's heart.

In Prague, beer is a way of life – among the varieties, Pilsner Urquell is one of the most distinctive Czech beers; Budvar is not to be confused with its American counterpart, Budweiser

Hotels and Accommodation

Prague today offers a better and more appealing choice of rooms than in the past, although prices are barely different to those in Berlin or Paris. Some 'state-of-the-art' modern hotels have also opened, in addition to an appealing collection of pensions.

Outdoor café at the Grand Evropa

Prices

Most hotels have now switched to the Western star system of grading, although it will be some time before service and accommodation fully meet Western standards for each category. In general, hotels are still expensive for what they offer. Private accommodation now provides a pleasant and economic alternative.

The following is an indication of what one might expect to pay for a double hotel room in Prague at the time of writing. Inflation and renovation costs will certainly increase prices. Breakfast is not always included, and hotels in the bottom two categories may have rooms without en suite bathrooms. Below the 5-star, the star rating requires flexible interpretation. Some hotels may still demand payment in hard currency.

- ★   up to 1,500kč
- ★★   1,500–2,999kč
- ★★★   3,000–4,999kč
- ★★★★   5,000–7,999kč
- ★★★★★ 8,000kč or above

Private accommodation is usually better value than a modest hotel, although in some cases, facilities may have to be with a family; in others, the hospitality may overwhelm the faint-hearted. Prices start at around 400kč per person. Rooms in the seasonally-rented college dormitories are cheaper, though still about 150–300kč per person.

The Diplomat Hotel has business people in mind, but all are welcome

Location

The hotels around the core of old Prague (Staré Město, Nové Město, Malá Strana) are almost all expensive. A few new luxury hotels have been built further out, but all of them have good communications to the centre. Prague retains a fair mix of residential and business properties in and around the old heart of the city, which means that it is usually possible to find private accommodation near the centre (check the hotel map to find out exactly where the room on offer is located).

Motels, camping sites, and youth hostels are on the periphery, or just outside the city. However, main arteries with buses or trams run close to most of them, and access to the centre of town is reasonably easy.

Booking

Trying to book a hotel direct can be a frustrating business and is not always reliable. Try the following websites for listings, and online booking for a huge list of hotels, pensions, hostels, and rooms for rent, to suit all budgets (*www.pis.cz* and *www.ave.cz*).

Travellers may still sometimes be told that Prague is 'fully booked' – apparently for a whole season. This could be technically true, in the sense that many of the city's hotels which are in the middle to upper price range are often block-booked a year ahead by package tour operators. There will still be accommodation available elsewhere.

Thomas Cook

Travellers who purchase their travel tickets from a Thomas Cook network location are entitled to use the services of any other Thomas Cook network location, free of charge, to make hotel reservations.

Reaching for the skies, the Forum Hotel in Vyšehrad

Booking Agencies in Prague

If you have arrived in Prague without a booking (or wish to change the hotel you have), there are now a lot of agencies that can help you find accommodation. You will also be offered rooms to rent by individuals at the Main Railway Station and at Holešovice Railway Station. Clearly, it is essential to check that the rooms are centrally located, or close to public transport – but you rent these at your own risk. AVE has an excellent accommodation service at both stations. A few other agencies include:

Agentura STOP CITY Pensions, rooms, and hotels (*www.stopcity.com*).

Prague Bed and Breakfast for hotels, studios, and apartments (*www.praguebedandbreakfast.com*).

Hotels Czeck hotels and other accommodation in the Czeck Republic (*www.hotelsczeck.com*).

Hotels in Prague online booking for comfortable and central hotels (*www.hotels.source.cz*).

Hotely v České Republice Accommodation in both Prague and the region (*www.hotely-on-line.cz/seznam*).

Luxury Hotels

The shortage of hotel beds at the luxury end of the market was already being remedied under the Communist regime, with an eye to the foreign business traveller. In recent years, several luxury hotels have been built. Among this are the **Marriott** (*tel: (02) 2182 1111*), the **Four Seasons** (*tel: (02) 2142 7000*), and the **Radisson SAS Hotel Praha** (*tel: (02) 2423 5390*) – the last in a superbly renovated Art Deco building.

A formal welcome at Hotel Atrium

Traditional Hotels

Sadly, only a few of the old-style hotels have retained real character and authentic decor. The best preserved of the Art Nouveau hotels are the truly shabby **Evropa** (*tel: (02) 2422 8117*), and the **Art Nouveau Pařiž** (*tel: (02) 2419 5195*), but they are difficult to book. An atmospheric little hotel is **U Tří Pštrosů** (*tel: (02) 2451 0779*) in a Renaissance house at the Malá Strana end of Charles Bridge. There are a number of other traditional hotels that tend to be clustered round the centre: the friendly **Casa Marello** (*tel: (02) 231 1230*), **Kampa** (*tel: (02) 5732 0508*), **Esplanade** (*tel: (02) 2421 1715*), and **Pařiž** (*tel: (02) 2219 3111*) are all in the city centre.

Botels

Staying on the Vltava sounds appealing, but the reality may be otherwise. There are three 'botels': the **Admirál** (*tel: (02) 5732 1302*) is the best of the bunch.

Pensions/Small Hotels
Pensions and cheaper modern hotels are mostly some way from the centre. Many are located in Prague 6 and 2.

Seasonal Hotels
Some college dormitories are turned into seasonal hotels. *Tel: (02) 2482 6662; e-mail: hostel@travellers.cz*

Youth Hostel
For bookings contact CKM, Žitná 12 (with your membership card). *Tel: (02) 29 12 40, www.ckm.cz* Also contact **Travellers Hostels,** all of which are centrally located. *Tel: (02) 2482 6662; e-mail: hostel@travellers.cz*

A taste of classic Prague

On Business

Some in the Czech Republic hope it is on track to join the EU in (potentially) 2004, and certainly Prague business life is increasingly cosmopolitan. Most former state organisations have been privatised, or are adapting themselves to life in a competitive market environment. Bohemia and Moravia offer the most attractive investment possibilities for the future. Certainly, investors continue to be attracted to its central location, cheap but highly qualified workforce, and attractive investment incentives. (*For more information*, see www.czeckinvest.com)

Čedok tourist agency offers many services

Business Hours
Most offices start at 8am and close at 6pm. Ministries in Prague are open 8am–4pm, Monday to Friday. Banks are generally open 8am–4pm, Monday to Friday, but some in the city centre have longer hours and close for an hour at lunchtime.

Conference Centres and Trade Fairs
Conferences are most prominently held at the Prague Congress Centre (or KCP), which hosted the World Bank/IMF conference in 2000 with considerable aplomb. Trade fairs are held at the main Prague venue: the Výstaviště complex in Holešovice, Prague 7 (metro line C to Nádraží Holešovice, trams 5, 12, and 17 to Výstaviště). Brno is the major trade fair city. Contact BVV (*tel: (05) 4115 1111* or *www.bvv.cz*) for details.

Etiquette
Wearing a suit is almost obligatory for the businessman here, so a more casual mode of dress can be taken as implying lack of seriousness. Czechs are punctilious in matters of formal courtesy, always shaking hands on meeting and at leave-taking. Punctuality is also very important.

Money
The *Prague Post* is a weekly newspaper, published on Wednesdays. It has commerce-oriented articles in its finance section, and gives the current exchange rates.

The Czech koruna (crown) (kč) is fully convertible.

Secretarial and Interpreter Services
Regus (*www.regus.com*) offers full office and secretarial services to those new to the scene. (Klimentská 46, Nové Město, *tel: (02) 2185 1055*.)

There are also ample human resources and recruitment agencies, only too eager to offer their assistance.

Check the *Prague Book of Lists*, published by the *Prague Business Journal*, for company listings (*www.pbj.cz*).

By Rail

From Lonc
hours, accc
direct rout
Dover, Osto
Informatio
European 1
Station, Lo;
848848).
Timetabl
internation
the *Thomas*
updated mc
branches of
by telephon
Internatic
railway corr
from Vienna
and Berlin,]
other Germa
Warsaw, and
in Prague at
Railway Stat
Nádraží Prak
on the Metrc
are valid for
Republic.

Camping

For informat
Apple Garde
Easy city-cen
etc. Very chea
Šeberov 20, F
3507; *www.ap*
Open: *Easter–*
Camp Dara 1
For simple ter
showers, toile
Trojska 129, F
0482; *www.vo*
Metro: *Holešo*

Translation and Interpreting

Organisations offering interpreting
services include:
ArtLingua: Myslikova 6, *tel: (02) 2491
8058; fax: 24921715; www.artlingua.cz*
Skřívánek: For translation and
interpretation services. Na dolinách 20,
Podoli (Prague 4), *tel: (02) 4143 0022;
www.skrivanek.cz*
Finist: Interpretation and translation are
on the menu.
Jurgmannova 24, Nové Město, *tel: (02)
2494 6365/6; www.finist.cz*

Telefax/Telegram/Telephone

At the Main Post Office at Jindříšká 14
(open 24 hours). *See also pp188–9.*

Courier

International courier services – **DHL**

(*tel: 0800 103000, www.dhl.cz*); local
messenger services by **Messenger**
(14001), *www.messenger.cz*
Try local listings (*www.pbj.cz*) for other
courier agencies.

Photocopying

Possibly the best Prague copy service is
C-Copy Centrum, on Opletalova 5
(*tel: (02) 2421 2110*), which features
pick-up and delivery services.
Otherwise, you'll find good copy shops
at the bottom of Vinohradská, and
opposite Nová Scěna on Národní.

Office Supplies

These are really ubiquitous. Try Tesco
or any of the family-run *papírnictvis.*
Makro (out-of-town) offers wholesale
prices, too.

Trade exhibitions are held at the U Hybernů Centre

P r

Arri

For

A va

trave

Sout

(obt

valid

By A

Ruzy

Czech

bus se

termi

to 7p

will d

Pragu

opera

Keeping u

ACKNOWLEDGEMENTS

Thomas Cook wishes to thank the photographers, picture libraries, and other organisations for the loan of the photographs reproduced in this book, to whom copyright in the photographs belongs.

CHRIS BARTON 1, 2, 18b, 20, 21a, 21b, 22a, 22b, 23, 59, 74b, 77, 98, 100b, 151a, 152a, 163, 164, 170
ISIFA 13, 14a, 16, 17, 24, 29, 43, 96, 97, 99, 100a, 108, 110, 115, 148, 157, 160a
PICTURES COLOUR LIBRARY 8, 40, 65, 91b, 121, 124, 154, 177, back cover top left
NEIL SETCHFIELD 12, 18a, 53a, 109, 158b, 173a, 174a.

The remaining pictures are held in the AA PHOTO LIBRARY and were taken by JON WYAND, with the exception of pages 5, 28, 39, 49, 58, 64, 68, 69, 75, 91a, 95, 105, 107b, 113, 114, 119, 125, 131, 151b, 160b, 165, 189, which were taken by ANTONY SOUTER.

FOR LABURNUM TECHNOLOGIES

Design Director	Alpana Khare	**Photo Editor**	Radhika Singh
Series Director	Razia Grover	**DTP Designers**	Neeraj Aggarwal, .
Editors	Madhavi Singh, Rajeev Jairam,		Harish Aggarwal
	Deepshikha Singh		

Updating and additional research on this edition was done by Susie Lunt.
Thanks to Marie Lorimer for the Index.